Commendations for Big Themes of the Bible

"Jon Morales is one of the brightest young stars in the evangelical firmament, and *Big Themes of the Bible* reveals why. In it, he highlights the narrative coherence of the Bible, the relationship of the Old and New Testaments, and the importance of the church. He connects everything to Jesus's message in a way that is accessible and helpful for college students, laypeople, and ministers. Highly recommended."

—*Bruce Riley Ashford, professor of theology and culture, Southeastern Baptist Theological Seminary*

"Starting with an anecdotal story of six blind men, Morales gradually opens the reader's eyes by tracing six big themes through the Bible. This book is an exercise in *seeing*—seeing and understanding the whole of the Christian story in the Bible. Morales has given us something accessible, informative, relevant, delightful!"

—*Cornelis Bennema, academic dean and senior lecturer in New Testament, Union School of Theology, Wales, UK*

"Jon Morales offers a readable and informative tour through several prominent biblical themes. The Bible is a big book, and Morales offers cogent and concise explanations as to what it is really about. A terrific resource for Bible studies!"

—*Michael F. Bird, academic dean and lecturer in theology, Ridley College, Melbourne, Australia*

"*Big Themes of the Bible* is a wonderful gift for today's church. Jon Morales writes with wit, wisdom, and faithfulness to Scripture that cultivates a love for God's Word. Today's disciple faces the daunting task of bearing witness in a post-Christian culture. If we are going to effectively call people into the better story of the gospel, it is essential that we know the comprehensive story of the Bible. *Big Themes* helps us do just that."

—*Chris Brooks, senior pastor, Woodside Bible Church, Troy, MI, and radio host, Moody Radio's* Equipped with Chris Brooks

"*Big Themes of the Bible* offers a beautiful survey of six major subjects in the Bible—creation, forgiveness, people, presence, yoke, and healing—that is clear and accessible. Tying both the Old Testament and the New Testament together, this book points to the unifying message of Jesus. For the new believer or the more experienced leader-servant in a church, *Big Themes of the Bible* will encourage you to grow in your walk with God and in the knowledge of his Word."

—*Tara Dew, adjunct professor in the Ministry Wives Certificate Program, New Orleans Baptist Theological Seminary*

"Jon Morales's *Big Themes of the Bible* is a masterful combination of deep thinking, careful research, pointed application, and a call to transformation. The careful reader is sure to ponder deeply, stand in awe, and weep over the grace of God in Christ as presented in this volume. It is a masterful treasure for both the seeker and the servant. I consider it a must-read for those who want clarity about our need for the gospel and Jesus's accomplishment for us."

—*L. Scott Kellum, professor of New Testament and Greek, Southeastern Baptist Theological Seminary*

"The story of God redeeming his people is a powerful, gripping, and yet simple story. Indeed, we sometimes overcomplicate its truths to the point that we lose our wonder over the grace of God. *Big Themes of the Bible* seeks to present that story clearly and concisely by focusing on the themes of creation, forgiveness, people, presence, yoke, and healing. Central to these themes is Jesus Christ, to whom the author directs us over and over again. Dr. Morales wants us to see more of Jesus, and he accomplishes that goal. You will find this book both informative and inspiring."

—*Chuck Lawless, vice president for spiritual formation and ministry centers, dean of doctoral studies, Richard and Gina Headrick Chair of World Missions, and professor of evangelism and missions, Southeastern Baptist Theological Seminary*

"This book by Morales is simple, yet profound. By tracing six central themes, he is able to accurately and skillfully present an overview of the message of the Bible. This book is not mere Christian fluff but is written by someone with a firm grasp of the Bible and a shepherd's heart. A great addition to the Hobbs College Library series."

—*Benjamin L. Merkle, professor of New Testament and Greek, Southeastern Baptist Theological Seminary*

"To write an introduction to the main themes of the Bible in just a hundred pages is a difficult task, but Morales has succeeded admirably. Not only does this book handle Scripture faithfully, but it is also clear, concise, interesting, engaging, and inspiring. I highly recommend it to anyone seeking to get a grasp of basic Christian beliefs."

—*Charles L. Quarles, research professor of New Testament and biblical theology and Charles Page Chair of Biblical Theology, Southeastern Baptist Theological Seminary*

Commendations for Hobbs College Library

"This series honors a wonderful servant of Christ with a stellar lineup of contributors. What a gift to the body of Christ! My hope and prayer is that it will be widely read and used for the glory of God and the good of his Church."

—Daniel L. Akin, president, Southeastern Baptist Theological Seminary

"This series is a must-have, go-to resource for everyone who is serious about Bible study, teaching, and preaching. The authors are committed to the authority of the Bible and the vitality of the local church. I am excited about the kingdom impact of this much-needed resource."

—Hance Dilbeck, executive director, Baptist General Convention of Oklahoma

"I am very excited about the dynamic leadership of Dr. Heath Thomas and his vision of the Hobbs College Library at Oklahoma Baptist University that he is developing. Through his work as dean of the Hobbs College of Theology, this 21-volume set of books will ascend the theological understanding of laypeople, church leaders, pastors, and bi-vocational pastors. Therefore, I want to encourage you to participate in this vision that will equip your church to make a greater difference for Jesus Christ in your community and around the world."

—Ronnie Floyd, president, the Southern Baptist Convention Executive Committee

"This series offers an outstanding opportunity for leaders of all kinds to strengthen their knowledge of God, his word, and the manner in which we should engage the culture around us. Do not miss this opportunity to grow as a disciple of Jesus and as a leader of his church."

—Micah Fries, senior pastor, Brainerd Baptist Church, Chattanooga, TN

"The Hobbs College Library is a perfect way to help people who want to grow in the basics of their faith. Whether you are a layperson or longtime pastor, this tool will help give you the theological base needed for ministry today. I highly recommend this tremendous resource to anyone wanting to deepen their understanding of Scripture."

—Jack Graham, pastor, Prestonwood Baptist Church, North TX, and former president, the Southern Baptist Convention

"The best resources are those that develop the church theologically while instructing her practically in the work of the Great Commission. Dr. Thomas has assembled an impressive host of contributors for a new set of resources that will equip leaders at all levels who want to leave a lasting impact for the gospel. Dr. Hobbs exemplified the pastor-leader-theologian, and it's inspiring to see a series put out in his name that so aptly embodies his ministry and calling."

—J.D. Greear, pastor, The Summit Church, Raleigh-Durham, NC, and president, the Southern Baptist Convention

BIG THEMES
OF THE BIBLE

HOBBS COLLEGE LIBRARY

BIG THEMES
OF THE BIBLE

Grasping the Heart
of Jesus's Message

JON MORALES

HEATH A. THOMAS, *Editor*

OBU

ACADEMIC

NASHVILLE, TENNESSEE

Big Themes of the Bible

Copyright © 2021 by Jon Morales

Published by B&H Academic
Nashville, Tennessee

ISBN: 978-1-0877-1298-7

Dewey Decimal Classification: 220.076
Subject Heading: JESUS CHRIST / GOD / PROVIDENCE
AND GOVERNMENT OF GOD

Printed in the United States of America
1 2 3 4 5 6 7 8 9 10 BP 26 25 24 23 22 21

For Anna

You said, "I do."

Everything else is a footnote.

Contents

Acknowledgments   *xiii*

About the Library   *xv*

Introduction: People and Elephants Are Not Trees   *1*

1. Creation   *9*

2. Forgiveness   *23*

3. People   *39*

4. Presence   *59*

5. Yoke   *75*

6. Healing   *89*

Epilogue: People as Trees   *99*

Name and Subject Index   *101*

Scripture Index   *105*

Acknowledgments

This book, like everything else that is good in my life, is the result of kindness—the kindness of God and friends.

Dr. Heath Thomas welcomed me into the PhD program at Southeastern and then invited me to write this volume. Thank you for your vote of confidence. I wholeheartedly affirm your vision for this series.

The team at B&H Academic has been a joy to work with. I'm thankful to Chris Thompson, Sarah Landers, Audrey Greeson, and Jessi Wallace for improving the work, clarifying many sentences, and seeing the project through to completion.

My professors—Jeff Purswell, John Frame, Scott Swain, Charles E. Hill, L. Scott Kellum, Charles L. Quarles, and many others—through instruction and example awakened my passion to read and study carefully the Scriptures.

My friend Steve Zarrilli demonstrates the rare humility that makes pastoral ministry about Jesus and not about the many lesser things we often choose.

Mark Goralewski, Jake Jakubek, and Andrea Dell are dear friends who have come to know Christ through the ministry of my local church. Your vibrant faith inspires me.

The staff and church family at Woodside Royal Oak have embraced me and my family with much grace.

My children Rayne, Jett, Piper, and Saylor are gems. I call them my five fine pearls (their mom is the fifth, but she's really the first). I love holding your hands around the dinner table.

Finally, I thank God for my wife, Anna. She alone has journeyed with me for the last twenty-one years. That's a lot of time to see a whole lot of gunk. Yet your kindness and faithfulness to me grow sweeter each year. I'm so grateful we both feel strongly about our shared mission in Christ.

About the Library

The Hobbs College Library equips Christians with tools for growing in the faith and for effective ministry. The library trains its readers in three major areas: Bible, theology, and ministry. The series originates from the Herschel H. Hobbs College of Theology and Ministry at Oklahoma Baptist University, where biblical, orthodox, and practical education lies at its core. Training the next generation was important for the great Baptist statesman Dr. Herschel H. Hobbs, and the Hobbs College that bears his name fosters that same vision.

The Hobbs College Library: Biblical. Orthodox. Practical.

Introduction:
People and Elephants Are Not Trees

There is a popular story of Indian origin about six blind men and an elephant. One version of the story goes like this.[1]

> It was six men of Indostan
> To learning much inclined,
> Who went to see the Elephant
> (Though all of them were blind),
> That each by observation
> Might satisfy his mind.
>
> The first approached the Elephant,
> And happening to fall
> Against his broad and sturdy side,
> At once began to bawl:
> "God bless me! but the Elephant
> Is very like a wall!"
>
> The second, feeling of the tusk,
> Cried, "Ho, what have we here,

---

[1] This public domain version of the poem is by John Godfrey Saxe.

So very round and smooth and sharp?
To me 'tis mighty clear
This wonder of an Elephant
Is very like a spear!"

The third approached the animal,
And happening to take
The squirming trunk within his hands,
Thus boldly up and spake:
"I see," quoth he, "the Elephant
Is very like a snake!"

The fourth reached out an eager hand,
And felt about the knee
"What most this wondrous beast is like
Is mighty plain," quoth he:
"'Tis clear enough the Elephant
Is very like a tree!"

The fifth, who chanced to touch the ear,
Said: "E'en the blindest man
Can tell what this resembles most;
Deny the fact who can,
This marvel of an Elephant
Is very like a fan!"

The sixth no sooner had begun
About the beast to grope,
Than seizing on the swinging tail
That fell within his scope,

"I see," quoth he, "the Elephant
Is very like a rope!"

And so these men of Indostan
Disputed loud and long,
Each in his own opinion
Exceeding stiff and strong,
Though each was partly in the right,
And all were in the wrong.

Each of the blind men, unable to see the whole, mistook the elephant for a wall, a spear, a snake, a tree, a fan, or a rope. The moral of the story is clear. Every world religion has part of the truth, but no religion (and no one) has the whole truth. This story captures well the spirit of our age. Truth is relative: *You have one piece. I have one piece. But nobody sees the whole.*

Except that the story makes the exact opposite point! Somebody sees the whole. Somebody knows that the elephant is not a wall, a spear, or a rope. Somebody knows that the blind men are partly right and partly wrong. Who? Who sees the whole? The narrator, the one telling the story. He sees fully. He knows what the elephant looks like. The story's title should be "Six Blind Men, an Elephant, and a Narrator Who Sees Just Fine"!

This story is a great apologetic not against but for the Christian faith.[2] What the Christian faith claims is not that Christians see clearly and know the truth fully. On the contrary, the Bible agrees with the story that humankind is blind. Moreover, the Bible also agrees with the story that reality is a whole, not a disparate tree, spear, or fan lying around. Finally, Scripture agrees with the story

---

[2]   Tim Keller, *The Reason for God: Belief in an Age of Skepticism* (New York: Riverhead, 2008), 9, says, "This illustration backfires on its users."

3

that there is a narrator who exists on a different plane from the rest of blind humanity.

But the main difference between this story and Scripture is that in Scripture the narrator enters our plane of existence, interacts with us, and restores our sight. Jesus Christ alone sees clearly and knows exhaustively. By giving us new information and experiences, he cures us step by step of our blindness. The book you now hold in your hands is an exercise in seeing.

Eye Problems

Around the midpoint of the Gospel of Mark, the themes of blindness and receiving sight become prominent. A blind man is brought to Jesus. Jesus spits on the man's eyes and, after putting his hands on him, asks, "Do you see anything?" The man says, "I see people—they look like trees walking." His response prompts Jesus to place his hands on the man one more time, and the story continues, "The man looked intently and his sight was restored and he saw everything clearly" (Mark 8:23–25).

People and elephants are not trees. The blind man goes from blindness to distorted eyesight to clear vision. Seeing clearly required Jesus and more than one touch. This man becomes a living parable of the blindness in Jesus's disciples. Just before the incident with the blind man, Mark records the following account between Jesus and his disciples:

> The disciples had forgotten to take bread and had only
> one loaf with them in the boat. Then he gave them strict
> orders: "Watch out! Beware of the leaven of the Pharisees
> and the leaven of Herod." They were discussing among
> themselves that they did not have any bread. Aware of

this, he said to them, "Why are you discussing the fact you have no bread? Don't you understand or comprehend? Do you have hardened hearts? Do you have eyes and not see; do you have ears and not hear? And do you not remember?" (Mark 8:14–18)

The disciples were worried because they had gotten into a boat with Jesus and forgotten to bring enough bread. Jesus told them, "Watch out! Beware of the yeast of the Pharisees and the yeast of Herod." The Pharisees represented the religious authorities, and Herod was the local political ruler on behalf of Rome. Jesus was saying to them, "Because you're with me, you're a target. Be careful." But the disciples' minds were on the bread they'd forgotten!

Here's the thing. The disciples had seen Jesus calm a raging storm and heal countless numbers of people, and do many other things they had never seen before, including the feeding of five thousand people and four thousand people out of a few loaves of bread, which explains Jesus's dismay with them. He said, "Why are you discussing the fact you have no bread? Don't you understand or comprehend? Do you have hardened hearts? Do you have eyes and not see?"

What's his point? It is this: our eyes fail to work properly.

A Question of Identity

After the healing of the blind man, the next episode in Mark reveals that the crowds also were blind in their understanding of Jesus's identity. The crowds, the disciples, the man—all were blind—and Jesus was determined to expose their blindness. He asked a question about identity—*his* identity. "Who do people say that I am?" The disciples answered that people had various opinions. Some said

Jesus was John the Baptist; others, Elijah; others, one of the prophets. Jesus was not satisfied with these answers, so he asked them
point-blank, "But you, who do you say that I am?" Peter answered,
"You are the Messiah" (Mark 8:29). At that point, Jesus began to
teach his disciples that he would be killed.

The perception of both the blind man and the crowds was
impaired. People are not trees, and Jesus is not just a prophet. He
is the Messiah. What's more, he is the Messiah who came to die.
And once the disciples understood and embraced this, along with
the reason for his death, their eyesight would be restored and they
would see everything clearly. But not in one touch. Step by step,
Jesus revealed his identity and unveiled their eyes so they could see
clearly.

Seeing the Whole

Imagine if, after the first touch, the blind man had said, "I see people, and they look just fine. They're walking, smiling, and look
great! Thank you, Jesus." But the whole time they looked to him
like trees. Jesus's question required honesty. Do you *see* anything?
What Jesus was after was the man's ability to see. And the honest
answer allowed Jesus to give the man the additional help he needed.

The central claim of the Christian faith is that Jesus is the Son of
God, who died and rose again in order to save his people from their
sins and heal God's creation. This is the gospel. His achievement—
his victory—becomes ours when we trust in him. All of this will be
unpacked in the following pages.

This gospel, however, is difficult to receive, not because of what
we must do, but because of what we must admit, that we need help.
This volume (as the rest of the volumes in the series) offers help in
understanding Jesus and the Christian Scriptures. My attempt is not

to be exhaustive. There are more big themes in the Bible than space in these pages. My goal is to simplify and to whet your appetite. The Bible is bulky; to many it feels uninviting, not unlike Tolstoy's *War and Peace*. Yet Scripture's many details and chapters become delightful once we grasp the heart of Jesus's message. People are not trees, and the Bible is not an encyclopedia. Encyclopedic in scope, yes. But first we must see the whole.

The themes highlighted in this volume attempt an overview that gives the reader a sense of the whole. What's more, it will soon become clear that Jesus Christ is the central figure who holds the many themes together. He's the narrator who sees the whole, enters our plane of existence, interacts with us, and restores our sight.

CHAPTER 1

Creation

I n the middle of a controversy about divorce, Jesus challenged his adversaries, "'Haven't you read,' he replied, 'that he who created them in the beginning made them male and female'?" (Matt 19:4). He was quoting from Gen 1:27 and then quoted Gen 2:24, "For this reason a man will leave his father and mother and be joined to his wife, and the two shall become one flesh" (Matt 19:5). Notice that he argued by going to the first few chapters of Genesis, where we find the biblical account of creation.

In our day, it is not uncommon to find many who avoid the Old Testament and consider it either unhelpful in understanding the Christian faith or harmful in evangelism. They prefer to focus on Jesus. But Jesus did not simply focus on Jesus. The Hebrew Scriptures were his Bible, and Genesis provided him with one of the most important themes we find in all of Scripture—that God is the Creator.

Since at least the nineteenth century, people have been coming to the opening chapters of Genesis with the wrong questions. How old is the earth? How long were the creation days? How about evolutionary theory? These are good questions but not the questions people were asking 3,000 and 4,000 years ago in the ancient Near East. Armed with the wrong questions, people miss the point and beauty of the first few chapters of Scripture.

Imagine that you invite someone from a foreign country who has never heard of American football to come and watch the Super Bowl with you and your family. You're very excited about the game. Your team made it to the Super Bowl. Your fifty-inch HD TV is ready to go. The snacks are superb. You're wearing your team's jersey. The day has come! And the game starts. And you're the kind of person who zeroes in on the game; you tune out everything else so you can be fully in the moment. Now your friend is sitting next to you, and he begins to ask you question after question. "What are the shoulder pads the players are wearing made of? Why do so many players have long hair? Is that a rule? Is it to look menacing like Vikings? I like that! Why do they stop the game so often? I don't like that! How long is the field? . . ."

What are all those questions doing for your enjoyment of the game? They're ruining it. These are the wrong questions about the game. They do not fit the occasion. Likewise, the questions Genesis answers are not *how* questions: How long are the creation days? How old is the earth? Genesis 1–3 answers *why* questions, and *why* questions are always more exciting and significant. Think about it. What's more significant and exciting to a husband? How his bride got to the altar on his wedding day, or *why* she got to the altar on his wedding day?

Why is there something rather than nothing? Why are we here? Why is life so difficult and puzzling? Genesis answers these questions and many more.

What Beginning?

The Bible opens with ten words that are as poetic as they are potent: "In the beginning God created the heavens and the earth" (Gen 1:1). These words were written for us, but first they were written to the people of Israel poised to enter the land of Canaan more than 3,000 years ago. Both the land of Canaan, in Israel's future, and the land of Egypt, in Israel's past, were filled with people who worshiped many gods. So Moses makes clear to Israel that they are in the middle of a story, a story with a beginning and moving toward an end. In the beginning of their story, which is also the beginning of the universe, there is one God, not many.

Notice what Moses did not say: "In the beginning many gods." Or, "In the beginning we." Or, "In the beginning mother nature." Or, "There was no beginning." He said, "In the beginning God."[1]

Did you know that until 1964 the prevailing theory of the origin of the universe in scientific circles was that the universe had no origin? It was called the steady-state hypothesis, which posited that the universe had always existed and would always exist in its current state. If as a scholar or scientist you tried to question the steady-state hypothesis, you would be ridiculed—much as many are ridiculed today for questioning evolutionary biology. The steady-state hypothesis stated: *there was no beginning to the universe.* This idea directly contradicted the first three words of the Bible, "In the beginning." No wonder many people in the twentieth century started saying, "Let's just focus on Jesus!" However, in the 1920s, some scientists began publishing articles showing evidence that the universe was expanding, and if it was expanding there must have been a beginning. But it took about four decades for the scientific consensus to do an about-face and affirm, "Yes, there must have been a beginning to the universe."[2]

---

[1] For a helpful introduction to Genesis, esp. the opening chapters, see Bruce K. Waltke, *An Old Testament Theology* (Grand Rapids: Zondervan, 2007), 173–208.

[2] You can read a fuller explanation of the steady-state hypothesis in Michael Guillen, *Amazing Truths: How Science and the Bible Agree* (Grand Rapids: Zondervan, 2015), 84–99.

The Creator: Father, Son, and Spirit

"In the beginning God created the heavens and the earth." Here I want you to learn a new word. I don't like obscure words, but this one is important. The word is *aseity,* from the Latin "a" (from) and "se" (self). Scripture teaches that God is an *aseity.* He is from himself. He depends on nothing or no one for his existence. He has always existed. He is self-sustaining. He has no needs whatsoever. This God, as Genesis puts it, created "the heavens and the earth," which is a merism, a totality represented by contrasting parts, as when we say "head to toe" to refer to the whole body. The biblical God created everything that exists.

But there is another important aspect of creation disclosed in the Scriptures. Creation was the activity of God the Father, God the Son, and God the Holy Spirit. Genesis hints at this work of the triune (three-in-one) God when it mentions God, but also "the Spirit of God . . . hovering over the surface of the waters" in Gen 1:2, and then the word of God, which is the agent by which all things were created. "Then God said, 'Let there be light,' and there was light" (v. 3). This word of God, we learn in the Gospel of John, is none other than Jesus Christ, God the Son (John 1:1, 14).[3]

Other Scriptures speak of the Spirit's agency in creation. Concerning all the creatures of the earth, the psalmist says, "When you send your breath [spirit], they are created" (Ps 104:30). One of Job's friends confessed, "The Spirit of God has made me, and the breath of the Almighty gives me life" (Job 33:4). God sent his Spirit, and

---

[3] Francis Watson, *Text, Church, and World: Biblical Interpretation in Theological Perspective* (Grand Rapids: Eerdmans, 1994), 137–53, develops a model for how Genesis 1 can be understood in trinitarian terms.

creatures came into being. As Michael Bird says, "The Spirit is the source of all energy, movement, and vitality in the universe."[4]

Similarly, a number of texts speak of Jesus's role in creation. "For everything was created by him, in heaven and on earth, the visible and the invisible, whether thrones or dominions or rulers or authorities—all things have been created through him and for him" (Col 1:16). "God has appointed him heir of all things and made the universe through him" (Heb 1:2). Jesus's early followers saw him calm a furious storm, heal the blind and lame, exorcise demons, multiply meager food rations into food for the masses, walk on water, change the molecular structure of water to become wine, and raise the dead. Such mastery over nature and supernatural forces, together with the testimony of God at Jesus's baptism and on the Mount of Transfiguration as well as the testimony of Jesus about himself, most profoundly related to his own sufferings, death, and resurrection, gave rise to the disciples' conviction that Jesus was one with God and thus the agent of creation. John says concerning Jesus, "All things were created through him, and apart from him not one thing was created that has been created" (John 1:3).

One of the biggest differences between biblical thought and other systems of thought is creation. The Bible teaches creation by the three-in-one God of everything that exists. In some Eastern religions, there is no clear distinction between god and creation. Everything and everyone is a part of the divine. In secular thought in the West, people often refer to "Mother Nature," which is an emotive way of saying that only material things exist. Everything we need comes from the earth. So Eastern thought says, *Everything is god*, and secular thought says, *Nothing is god*. Both erase the creator-creature distinction. In contrast, Scripture maintains that *God*

---

[4]   Michael F. Bird, *Evangelical Theology: A Biblical and Systematic Introduction* (Grand Rapids: Zondervan, 2013), 149.

alone is eternal, and he (Father, Son, and Spirit) created everything else. Although his creation depends on him and is related to him, the creation is not him.[5]

Look at the Birds

Related to creation is Scripture's teaching on *providence*. God created the world and did not abandon it. Everything God created is good, and those who are familiar with the account of Genesis 1 remember the constant refrain after God's word acts on the days of creation, "And it was good." Sadly, things did not remain good for long. The first humans made a fatal choice, and sin and death entered into earthly life. (We will explore these events in chapter 2.) But the earth remained God's, and his involvement and commitment to it are ever-present.

When God made himself known to Moses, he highlighted certain attributes of his character. "The LORD passed in front of [Moses] and proclaimed: The LORD—the LORD is a compassionate and gracious God, slow to anger and abounding in faithful love and truth, maintaining faithful love to a thousand generations, forgiving iniquity, rebellion, and sin" (Exod 34:6–7). There are many other things God could have said, and did say, but it was important that his people know him for his compassion, grace, slowness to anger, faithful love, truth, and willingness to forgive.

Many people today (and throughout history) do not see evidence of God's involvement in the world. Wars, famines, natural disasters, and the depth of human evil and suffering lead many to conclude that there is no God—or, if there is a God, he has forgotten the earth.

---

[5] For a primer on some of the worldviews that compete with the biblical worldview, see James W. Sire, *The Universe Next Door,* 5th ed. (Downers Grove, IL: Inter-Varsity, 2009).

Scripture, however, insists that the same God who created the universe is still committed to the earth, involved in it, and determined to bringing life and peace to it for all eternity. This is what it means for God to be "abounding in faithful love." Psalm 33 is a wonderful example of the many places in Scripture where God's people affirm God's involvement in their lives and in the world: "The earth is full of the LORD's unfailing love" (v. 5). The writer continues,

> The LORD frustrates the counsel of the nations;
> he thwarts the plans of the peoples.
> The counsel of the LORD stands forever,
> the plans of his heart from generation to generation.
> Happy is the nation whose God is the LORD—the people
> he has chosen to be his own possession!

> The LORD looks down from heaven;
> he observes everyone.
> He gazes on all the inhabitants of the earth
> from his dwelling place.
> He forms the hearts of them all;
> he considers all their works.
> A king is not saved by a large army;
> a warrior will not be rescued by great strength.
> The horse is a false hope for safety;
> it provides no escape by its great power.

> But look, the LORD keeps his eye on those who fear him—
> those who depend on his faithful love
> to rescue them from death
> and to keep them alive in famine.
> We wait for the LORD;

> he is our help and shield.
> For our hearts rejoice in him
> because we trust in his holy name.
> May your faithful love rest on us, LORD,
> for we put our hope in you. (vv. 10–22)

There is, indeed, an entire way of viewing life implicit in this psalm. God's plans and counsel stand forever, whereas the counsel of the nations is frustrated by him. God looks and considers the works of humanity and brings deliverance, not to those who set their hope on military, physical, or economic might, but on those who look to him and, specifically, to his faithful love to rescue them from death. "We wait for the LORD."

Jesus extended God's providence to his care for the birds of the air and the lilies of the field (Matt 6:26, 28). Of course, he was making a more important point. *If God feeds the birds and clothes the flowers, won't he do much more for you?* What's more, God causes the sun (lit. *his* sun, in Matt 5:45) to rise on the evil and the good and sends rain on the just and the unjust. Jesus was using God's generosity toward all persons to motivate his people not to be tribal in their love but to love even their enemies. God's care and involvement with all the people of the earth should make those who know him confident, not anxious, and generous, not mean or petty.[6]

Everything New

To go from creation to *new* creation omits the entirety of human history and may seem arbitrary. But it is not. For often the best way to understand the present is to look back, as we have done by going

---

[6]   Jerry Bridges, *Trusting God* (Colorado Springs, CO: NavPress, 2008), explores the providence of God in many biblical texts and with pastoral sensitivity.

to Genesis, but also to look forward, as we will by going briefly to Revelation.[7]

> Then I saw a new heaven and a new earth, for the first heaven and the first earth had passed away, and the sea was no more. I also saw the holy city, the new Jerusalem, coming down out of heaven from God, prepared like a bride adorned for her husband.
>
> Then I heard a loud voice from the throne: Look, God's dwelling is with humanity, and he will live with them. They will be his peoples, and God himself will be with them and will be their God. He will wipe away every tear from their eyes. Death will be no more; grief, crying, and pain will be no more, because the previous things have passed away.
>
> Then the one seated on the throne said, "Look, I am making everything new." (Rev 21:1–5)

As mentioned earlier, God is the Creator of everything that exists, and he has not abandoned his creation. At the very end of Scripture, we have a vision given to John, unveiling the situation of the Christian churches in Asia Minor at the end of the first century AD. This vision narrated their political and existential struggle from God's point of view. Things looked bleak on earth, so the Christians—but also the nations around them among whom the message of Jesus was spreading—needed the force and clarity of things in heaven. And Revelation is forceful.

For about 1,900 years, Christians have had a love-hate relationship with this book. Many find it confusing and scary. And it

---

[7] We will have more to say about new creation in the chapter on healing.

is scary, but we're scared of the wrong things in Revelation. People find scary the beasts, the four living creatures full of eyes, the horsemen of death, the earthquakes, the consuming fires, the locusts with lions' teeth. But do you know what's the scariest thing in Revelation? Jesus Christ—because he's in control of all those other things. In Revelation, Jesus Christ is not a baby. Neither is he on a cross, bleeding to death. He's alive. He's the "Living One." He says, "I was dead, but look—I am alive forever and ever, and I hold the keys of death and Hades" (Rev 1:18). All those other things are agents of death. That's why we fear them. But who holds the keys of death? Jesus himself.

In Revelation, Jesus comes to John in awesome appearance, his eyes like a flame of fire, and his voice like the roar of many waters. And he's in the midst of seven lampstands, which are the seven churches in Asia Minor, symbolically representing the universal church for all the ages (because seven is the number of *completeness*). We learn that Jesus is not just standing in the midst of the churches. He walks among them (Rev 2:1). The living, alive-forevermore, death-and-Hades-holding Christ walks with his eyes like flames of fire in the midst of his churches. His presence is both comforting and unsettling. He is with us, but he also has piercing vision. He knows our hearts. He knows us, and there is no hiding from his sight.

Unfortunately, the majesty and authority of Jesus as disclosed to us in Revelation are often missing from the mental picture many Christians have of Christ. "The LORD is my shepherd" must be balanced with "the Lion from the tribe of Judah" (Rev 5:5). His words to the churches in Revelation 2–3 should make most of us uncomfortable; they unmask a deep unbelief. But the reason he confronts our unbelief is that he wants us, individually and as churches, to conquer it. He wants us to conquer unbelief, so that we might enjoy the reward of his promises: the right to eat from the tree of life, to be unharmed by the second death, to receive from him a white stone with a new name, to shepherd the nations, to be dressed in white clothes, to be a pillar in God's temple and bear God's name, and to sit with him on his throne.[8] These promises have a future orientation and find final fulfillment in the new creation.

Where is your life headed? Where is the earth headed? Your answers to these questions will affect how you live every day. Our Creator has abandoned neither humanity nor the earth! "Look, I am making everything new." "Look, God's dwelling is with humanity." "Then I saw a new heaven and a new earth."[9] What happens between God's original creation and his new (and yet future) creation is the subject of the next few chapters; it's the subject of Genesis 3 all the way to Revelation 20. But it is good for the mind and heart to know the beginning and the end of the story because the middle can get quite convoluted. Contrary to the opinion of many, death is not the final chapter in human life. There is another death, the second death, and there is another life, resurrected life. Which one is our lot depends on how we answer the question, *Who is Jesus?* And then how we respond to him. But the purpose of God is to dwell with his people in the new earth. And when he does, death, grief, crying, and pain will be no more.

---

[8]   See Rev 2:7, 11, 17, 26–27; 3:5, 12, 21. Two short and insightful resources on Revelation are Michael J. Gorman, *Reading Revelation Responsibly: Uncivil Worship and Witness, Following the Lamb into the New Creation* (Eugene, OR: Wipf & Stock, 2011), and Richard Bauckham, *The Theology of the Book of Revelation* (Cambridge: Cambridge University Press, 1993).

[9]   Respectively, Rev 21:5, 3, 1.

One God

The Nicene Creed, a confession that all branches of Christianity have affirmed for nearly 1,700 years, begins this way: "We believe in one God, the Father Almighty, Maker of heaven and earth, and of all things visible and invisible." A number of important implications emerge from the doctrine of creation.

There Is One God

Israel's most foundational confession separated them from all other nations. It is found in Deut 6:4 and is known as the *Shema*. "Listen, Israel: The LORD our God, the LORD is one." As we have seen, with the coming of Jesus and the sending of the Holy Spirit, the New Testament reveals to us that God is Father, Son, and Spirit. In Matt 28:19, Jesus commands his disciples to baptize all new disciples "in the name of the Father and of the Son and of the Holy Spirit." Notice that it is *one name*, but that one name consists of Father, Son, and Spirit.

Many people today believe in many gods, or they affirm that every person is entitled to believe in his or her own god. Others believe that there is no god. But the witness of Scripture is that there is one God, and he is the Maker of heaven and earth.

God and His Creation Are Distinct

The most radical conception of ontology (the branch of philosophy that studies *being*) can be illustrated by two circles that do not touch, a bigger one above a smaller one.[10] The bigger circle represents God. The smaller circle represents the created universe. The

---

[10] Professor John Frame, following his mentor Cornelius Van Til, used to draw these two circles on the board in many of his classes at Reformed Theological Seminary in Orlando, FL.

diagram makes clear that (1) there is one God, not many or none, and (2) this God is not one with his creation. He is separate, distinct. Nature is not God. Humans are not God. Both come from God, but he alone is self-existent.

As a created being, the most important question I must ask is, *Who is my Creator?* If a personal, intelligent Creator made me, then I must find out, "Why was I made? What is the Creator's purpose for my life? Under what conditions do I and all other human beings flourish the most?" We are neither self-existent nor self-designed. We are not autonomous. The beginning words of the prayer Jesus taught us to say are "Our Father in heaven" (Matt 6:9). The universe has a sovereign, and we're not he. Therefore, the most profound self-discovery is to learn *who we are in light of who he is*.

God Is Involved with and Committed to the Renewal of His Creation

Although God is distinct from his creation, he is not distant. The greatest demonstration of his involvement and commitment to the earth was the sending of his Son, Jesus Christ, who came to bring people back to God. "For Christ also suffered for sins once for all, the righteous for the unrighteous, that he might bring you to God" (1 Pet 3:18). Why his suffering and death were necessary will be detailed in the next chapter. For now, it is important to see that the coming of Jesus is the most tangible intersection of heaven with earth. He came from above and made his dwelling among humankind, and he sent his Spirit among those who believe in him, so that we would know that we are never alone but are always under his guidance and surrounded by his presence. Politics, history, the economy, social institutions and trends, as well as the ins and outs of our lives—are all subject to the purposes of God in Christ for the remaking of the earth.

Our Lives Are Not Random but Have Meaning and Purpose

Because we exist by the purposeful creation of God, and not by chance, and because God has not abandoned his creation but is reclaiming it through the life and work of Jesus, we can rest assured that our lives, individually and collectively, have meaning and purpose. We seek beauty in nature and in our homes because God made things beautiful. We seek meaning in our work, even in our leisure, because God made us for work, and our work should inspire and make life better.

When people believe that they exist merely by the random and utterly impersonal collocation of chemicals, it is difficult to make sense of life. That's because our strongest attachments are utterly personal: a child, a parent, a friend. But when we know that the world is a gift from a personal God, our relationships and work can also be received and offered as a gift. And when we know that this personal God is renewing his creation and making his eternal dwelling with us, we are compelled to cherish the earth and demonstrate love to our fellow human beings. Why that task is so difficult for us is the subject of the next chapter, the next great theme of the Bible.

CHAPTER 2

Forgiveness

Picture this. A woman, an outcast, someone who carries the stigma of living beyond the norms of cultural acceptability and privilege. This woman finds out that Jesus is having dinner at the house of her opposite—a man of privilege, whose social circle writes the rules of cultural acceptability, of who's in and who's out. What does the woman do? She goes into the man's house and makes a fool of herself. "She brought an alabaster jar of perfume and stood behind [Jesus] at his feet, weeping, and began to wash his feet with her tears. She wiped his feet with her hair, kissing them and anointing them with the perfume" (Luke 7:37–38).

We cannot imagine anyone at Starbucks or anywhere else, for that matter, doing this. Yet in Jewish culture in first-century Palestine, hospitality norms included offering water for the guests' feet, a kiss, and even pouring oil on their heads. Certainly the woman's actions went beyond these conventions. She used her tears and her hair, and she's directing her affection to Jesus's feet. Think about it. Feet. In a place where people walked for miles and shared the dirt roads with animals: stinky, crusty, nasty feet. And there was little, at the time, that made Jesus special. No Da Vinci or Michelangelo paintings of him had been imprinted in the collective psyche. Jesus's feet were like any man's feet.

The woman went out on a limb, and the disdain, at least from the host, was pronounced. His name was Simon, and Simon looked down on the woman (because she was stigmatized) and on Jesus (because he let the woman near him).

Then Jesus addressed Simon. "A creditor had two debtors. One owed five hundred denarii, and the other fifty. Since they could not pay it back, he graciously forgave them both. So, which of them will love him more?" Simon answered, "I suppose the one he forgave more." And Jesus replied, "You have judged correctly" (Luke 7:41–43).

Jesus continued.

> Turning to the woman, he said to Simon, "Do you see this woman? I entered your house; you gave me no water for my feet, but she, with her tears, has washed my feet and wiped them with her hair. You gave me no kiss, but she hasn't stopped kissing my feet since I came in. You didn't anoint my head with olive oil, but she has anointed my feet with perfume. Therefore I tell you, her many sins have been forgiven; that's why she loved much. But the one who is forgiven little, loves little." Then he said to her, "Your sins are forgiven." (vv. 44–48)

"The one who is forgiven little loves little." Jesus made a connection that is not obvious to us. He tied the degree of our love to the degree of the forgiveness we've experienced. His point is not that some people need a lot of forgiveness while others need little. His point is that some people don't see their need for forgiveness while others do. (Remember, this book is an exercise in *seeing*.) And only those who see their need for forgiveness, and how great that need

is, will be forgiven; having experienced much forgiveness, they are then able to express much love.

By the end of this chapter, we will have asked and answered the following questions: What is forgiveness? Why is it required? How is it accomplished? Genesis 3 helps us understand the need for forgiveness.

A God of No

Genesis 1 and 2 give the biblical account of creation. Genesis 3 gives the biblical account of the fall of humankind. Many philosophical and religious systems assume that humanity is fallen. Broken. Twisted. Evil. In need of and desiring salvation.[1] Moreover, practical experience reveals to us that humankind is fallen: war, genocide, poverty, starvation, illness, turmoil—be it political, economic, racial, or social. Scholars vigorously disagree as to the cause and solution for our ills, but no argument is needed to convince the average person that the human race is desperately sick. We are destroying ourselves as well as the earth, our home.

The biblical account in Genesis 3 locates the loss of human wholeness and life to the time when we lost the voice of God for the voice of an impostor. That impostor was the serpent, a disguise for the Devil, who is presented later in Scripture as the prince of demons and whose origin is mysterious.[2] Let's explore this episode to bolster our theological understanding of the origin of the fallen human condition.

---

[1]   See Luc Ferry, *A Brief History of Thought: A Philosophical Guide to Living* (New York: Harper Perennial, 2003), 1–16, on how all religions and philosophical systems deal in the main with the question of salvation.

[2]   Theologians believe that between Genesis 1 and 3 a rebellion took place, based on 2 Pet 2:4. See, e.g., Wayne Grudem, *Systematic Theology: An Introduction to Biblical Doctrine* (Grand Rapids: Zondervan, 1994), 412–14.

In Gen 3:1–7 we read,

> Now the serpent was the most cunning of all the wild animals that the LORD God had made. He said to the woman, "Did God really say, 'You can't eat from any tree in the garden'?"
>
> The woman said to the serpent, "We may eat the fruit from the trees in the garden. But about the fruit of the tree in the middle of the garden, God said, 'You must not eat it or touch it, or you will die.'"
>
> "No! You will not die," the serpent said to the woman. "In fact, God knows that when you eat it your eyes will be opened and you will be like God, knowing good and evil." The woman saw that the tree was good for food and delightful to look at, and that it was desirable for obtaining wisdom. So she took some of its fruit and ate it; she also gave some to her husband, who was with her, and he ate it. Then the eyes of both of them were opened, and they knew they were naked; so they sewed fig leaves together and made coverings for themselves.

Notice how the serpent changes Eve's perception of God. The serpent said, "Did God really say, 'You can't eat from any tree in the garden'?" More literally his question is, "Did God actually say no to your eating of any tree in the garden?" Now, let's go back and look at what God had said. Genesis 2:16–17 says, "And the LORD God commanded the man, 'You are free to eat from any tree of the garden, but you must not eat from the tree of the knowledge of good and evil, for on the day you eat from it, you will certainly die.'"

Do you see the difference? God had said, "You are free to eat from any tree of the garden." Then he made one exception, the tree of the knowledge of good and evil. But the serpent said, "God said no to your eating of any tree in the garden." Of course, he was subtle and posed it as a question, but in the end he presented God as *a God of No*. And if you think about it, people tend to think of God as a God of No. A God of rules. A God who keeps the best things from them. God's command in Genesis 2:16 is incredibly generous, but the serpent made him appear severe and stingy.

How did Eve respond? By leaving some things out and adding some things in. She left out "God said" from her first statement. She said, "We may eat the fruit from the trees in the garden," but she should have said, "God said that we may eat the fruit from the trees in the garden." The change is subtle but significant, because she said "God said" only about the prohibition. Do you see? She said, "But about the fruit of the tree in the middle of the garden, God said, 'You must not eat it or touch it, or you will die.'" In her mind, God was present to forbid but not to give. In her mind, the prohibition came from God—the many trees just happened to be there.

She also left out the word *any* from Genesis 2:16, where God said, "You are free to eat from any tree." To the serpent, she said, "We may eat the fruit from the trees," but she left out the vast generosity in God's command: Eat from *any* tree! All this I have created, and it's for you!

Eve also added to the command. Look at what she says in Genesis 3:3, "But about the fruit of the tree in the middle of the garden, God said, 'You must not eat it or touch it, or you will die.'" God never said, "You must not touch it." So she made the command more stringent than God had made it.

As their dialogue continues, the serpent outright contradicts God's word. In Genesis 2:17, God had said, "But you must not eat

27

from the tree of the knowledge of good and evil, for on the day you eat from it, you will certainly die." But in Genesis 3:4, the serpent said, "No! You will not die." The serpent was no longer subtly introducing questions, changing a few words here and there. Now he plainly said the opposite of God's word. The serpent said, "You will not die."

Finally, the serpent made it sound as if God were keeping something good from Adam and Eve. "In fact, God knows that when you eat it your eyes will be opened and you will be like God, knowing good and evil" (v. 5).

The serpent never commanded the woman to eat of the tree God forbade, but his work of deception was done. God and his word seemed distant. What God had or had not said was no longer clear. The tree and the voice of the impostor were now closest to Eve. And so we read, "The woman saw that the tree was good for food and delightful to look at, and that it was desirable for obtaining wisdom. So she took some of its fruit and ate it; she also gave some to her husband, who was with her, and he ate it" (v. 6).

There was a progression in the tragic road from personal relationship with God to outright rebellion. Adam and Eve began in the garden with God. He created them and made a beautiful garden for them. He gave them to each other, provided meaningful work and ample provision. Everything was theirs to enjoy, except one tree. But then they began to listen to an impostor, the serpent, one with whom they had no previous relationship. He twisted God's words and introduced doubt. Then they left God out of the statement of provision. "We may eat the fruit from the trees in the garden," as if they—by their own power—had made the trees appear. Then they left out God's extreme generosity: "You are free to eat from any tree." They left out the word *any*. Then they added to God's command (he hadn't said, "you must not touch it"), so that they viewed him as severe, stingy, and restrictive. Finally, they listened to the serpent's direct contradiction of God's judgment when it said, "No! You will not die." After this dialogue, nothing stood between Adam and Eve and the forbidden tree—the place of strength, beauty, and wisdom they desired *apart from God.* Eve took of the fruit and ate. Adam took of the fruit and ate.

A Restless Creature

In the book *The Firm* by John Grisham, the main character, Mitch McDeere, is a young attorney (played by Tom Cruise in the movie) who gets a job with a law firm that appears to be too good to be true. What got him hooked on the firm were the usual perks: the high salary, the prestige, the stroking of his ego by the partners. What he didn't realize until later was that the firm was corrupt, and it began to control his life.

Suppose that during the interview process the firm had led with the following: "Okay, Mitch, we really like you, and we're going to pay you very well, but there are a couple of things you need to know about us. First, we're going to control your life. The words *privacy* or *personal time* don't exist in our world. We hope you're okay with that. Second, we're under investigation by the FBI. Now, sign here and here, and we'll see you on Monday. Welcome aboard." If they had led with those facts, would Mitch have taken the job? Only if he was a fool. But that's the thing about deception. It shows you only one side; on the other, it has "Death" written all over it.

As soon as Adam and Eve ate from the tree God had forbidden, their eyes were indeed opened—but what they saw, what they knew, was not what the serpent had promised. Something horrible had happened. They discovered that they were naked. Before they disobeyed God, they were naked and not ashamed (Gen 2:25). But now, they knew that they *were* naked, and they did not like it. They hurried to cover themselves. Their eyes were opened to their need for covering. They no longer felt comfortable with each other. The serpent had promised that they would become like God, but they were already like God, made in his image. Now they were not with God. They chose the voice of an impostor over the voice of God, and, in doing so, they lost him. They lost the relational peace, safety, and provision they had always known at his side. And the price of rebellion was the judgment of God.

You've read in novels or seen in movies the following scene many times. A husband and wife love each other and enjoy each other's presence in the home. The hallways are filled with pictures of their wedding, their trips, their many years together. A peculiar sweetness hangs in the air. And then the husband goes and undresses another woman and forsakes the wife of his youth. When he returns home, nothing's the same. The sweetness that hung in the air is gone. The very presence of his faithful wife makes him uncomfortable. The pictures of their wedding and their trips are reminders of his misdeed, his shame. And that's what we have in Genesis 3:8. "Then the man and his wife heard the sound of the LORD God walking in the garden at the time of the evening breeze, and they hid from the LORD God among the trees of the garden."

Adam and Eve had broken faithfulness with God, and now the very presence of God made them uncomfortable, so they hid. Think of how many times, prior to this incident, they must have heard the sound of the fullness of him who fills all in all, and the thrill and peace they would have felt. But now Adam could not feel safe with God in the garden, and he was afraid. All kinds of new emotions, negative ones, had come into his consciousness: fear, vulnerability, discomfort, shame. So he hid. And that is a good description of humankind from that point forward. Like Adam, we are restless creatures hiding from God.

Transgression Came through Eating

If Genesis 3:8 were the end of the Bible, the book would be very short. What follows, however, is a story of triumph, of love, of judgment, and of salvation. God came to Adam and Eve and confronted them. His first question to them was, "Where are you?" (Gen 3:9). This question is a word of grace, because it shows that God, like a shepherd after lost sheep, still wants relationship with Adam and Eve. But the road back to God would be long and the way hard. God listened to Adam and Eve before issuing judgment on them, as a just judge would do. Their lives, having known only good and peace, would now be marked by difficulty—in childbearing, relationships, work, and provision of that without which there is no life, food (Gen 3:9–19). From dust they had come and to dust they would return, and their home while sojourners on earth could no longer be the garden of Eden. God drove them out and blocked their access to the tree of life.

Many themes in Scripture reflect the human condition that has resulted from our first parents' rejection of and subsequent alienation from God. They include exile and our corresponding longing for home; death and our longing for life and permanence; poverty and our search for riches; exclusion, loneliness, and the desire for a healthy family; barrenness and our desire for progeny; evil and protracted conflict and our desire for safety and lasting peace. In the garden, Adam and Eve succumbed to the desire to be *like* God, but what made them human in the fullest sense was to be *with* God, living by his personal words.

The triumph of God came to humanity through a reversal of the very source of Adam and Eve's rebellion: food. The antidote came through the same channel the poison was delivered: the lips. In the judgment that God brings to our first parents, notice the repetition of one keyword in God's address to Adam.

> Because you listened to your wife and *ate* from the tree
> about which I commanded you "Do not *eat* of it":
> The ground is cursed because of you.
> You will *eat* from it by means of painful labor
> all the days of your life.
> It will produce thorns and thistles for you,
> and you will *eat* the plants of the field. You will *eat* bread
> by the sweat of your brow. (Gen 3:17–18, italics added)

The transgression came through eating; therefore the punishment came in humanity's effort to eat. Five times this keyword is repeated. Before their rebellion, Adam and Eve had worked and eaten from the garden without futility and frustration, without sweat, without thorns and thistles fighting against them. But rather than receiving the delight, wisdom, and good they believed the forbidden tree would offer, they found themselves exposed, confused, and banished from the presence of God. *You will eat bread by the sweat of your brow.*

Is there another kind of food?

A New Kind of Food

There is another "genesis" in the Bible, another beginning, and it takes place with the birth of Jesus Christ. In fact, in the first verse of the first chapter of the first book of the New Testament, Matthew uses that same Greek word, *genesis*, to refer to the account of the origin of Jesus Christ. In that same opening chapter, an angel tells Joseph that Mary's baby is to be named Jesus "because he will save his people from their sins" (Matt 1:21). How will this salvation that Jesus brings come about? The entire Gospel of Matthew tells the story. But there is an important event on the evening before Jesus's death that helps us connect the dots. Matthew narrates:

> As they were eating, Jesus took bread, blessed and broke it, gave it to the disciples, and said, "Take and eat it; this is my body." Then he took a cup, and after giving thanks, he gave it to them and said, "Drink from it, all of you. For this is my blood of the covenant, which is poured out for many for the forgiveness of sins." (Matt 26:26–28)

Remember what happened in Genesis when Adam and Eve abandoned God's word, listened to the voice of an impostor, and latched on to the one tree God told them not to eat from. "She took some of its fruit and ate it; she also gave some to her husband, who was with her, and he ate it" (Gen 3:6). *They took and ate from the tree that brought death.*

But in God's plan the death of Jesus was a giving of his body, so that when people take and eat from it, their sins might be forgiven. *He will save his people from their sins.* How? By providing for us a new tree from which to take and eat and live. "He himself bore our sins in his body on the tree; so that, having died to sins, we might live for righteousness. By his wounds you have been healed" (1 Pet 2:24). Christians take the communion, the Lord's Supper, because by faith we are eating a new kind of food—the body and blood of Jesus given for our forgiveness.[3]

---

[3] For understanding the crucifixion, see N. T. Wright, *The Day the Revolution Began: Reconsidering the Meaning of Jesus's Crucifixion* (New York: HarperCollins,

When Jesus began his ministry, he first went to the desert where he was tempted by the Devil. The Devil, however, did not approach him until *after* Jesus had fasted forty days and forty nights (Matt 4:2–3). The one who had come to save his people from their sins must demonstrate that the voice of the impostor has no sway over him; that hunger and need at the point of greatest human weakness do not weaken his resolve to honor God; that he knows that life is found in "every word that comes from the mouth of God" (v. 4). Jesus must prove that he will succeed where Adam and Eve failed, when they despised the word of God. And he did. Rather than allowing the voice of the impostor to steal Jesus's allegiance to God, Jesus fought the Devil with the very word of God—without adding to it or taking away, as Adam and Eve had done. In the end, weak but triumphant, Jesus sent the Devil away. "Go away, Satan! For it is written: Worship the Lord your God, and serve only him" (v. 10). What did Jesus consume in his moment of greatest human weakness? The word of God.[4]

John's Gospel records an instance where we get another window into Jesus's view of food. Jesus had been traveling and doing ministry as usual. He and his disciples were tired and hungry. When the disciples returned with food, they said to him, "Rabbi, eat something." And he said, "I have food to eat that you don't know about." And then he added, "My food is to do the will of him who sent me and to finish his work" (John 4:31, 32, 34). Adam and Eve had sought life apart from God. They wanted his gifts but neither his words nor his presence. Jesus, in contrast, fed on the will of God; as

---

2016); John Piper, *Fifty Reasons Why Jesus Came to Die* (Wheaton, IL: Crossway, 2006); Michael J. Gorman, *Cruciformity: Paul's Narrative Spirituality of the Cross* (Grand Rapids: Eerdmans, 2001).

[4] To deepen your conviction and understanding of the Bible as the word of God, see John Frame, *The Doctrine of the Word of God* (Phillipsburg, NJ: P&R, 2010).

a result, he can offer to us the food of forgiveness. Death came to our first parents and, through them, to the whole world, but life comes through Jesus to all who take and eat from his body. "I am the living bread that came down from heaven. If anyone eats of this bread he will live forever" (John 6:51).

Answering the Questions on Forgiveness

We are now able to answer the questions posed at the beginning of this chapter. What is forgiveness? Why is it required? How is it accomplished? Let's begin with the second question, *Why is forgiveness required?* Forgiveness is required because our first parents ignored the word of God and sought life apart from God, and every person after them has done the same.[5] This state of rebellion is what Scripture calls sin, and sin incurs the judgment of God. The biblical explanation for humanity's endless cycle of pain and death is that we live in rebellion and under judgment. Everyone can sense that things are not right with the world. What many cannot believe is that the reason for the world's ills lies in our estrangement from our Creator, and yet that is precisely Scripture's witness. We ate from the tree that made us rebels.

What then is forgiveness? Forgiveness is the canceling of our debt to God. It is God's bestowal of relationship to us, not treating us as our sins deserve, because our sins have been removed far from us. Forgiveness is the removal of God's righteous judgment that hung over us and the bestowal of blessing and life. When someone

---

[5]   Greg M. Epstein, *Good without God: What a Billion Nonreligious People Do Believe* (New York: Harper, 2009), defines humanism as being "good without God," xiii. He quotes on the dedication page a song of Humanistic Judaism by Rabbi Sherwin Theodore Wine: "Where is my light? My light is in me. Where is my hope? My hope is in me. Where is my strength? My strength is in me . . . and in you."

experiences the forgiveness of God, that person's spirit of rebellion no longer controls them. Instead of living in rebellion and under the judgment of death, the person forgiven by God relates to God in a relationship of love and lives eternally under his blessing.

How is forgiveness accomplished? Only through the death of Jesus. Jesus came to save his people from their sins by bearing their sins in his body on the tree, the cross. When someone by faith takes and eats of his body, that person is partaking of the One who gave his life for the forgiveness of sins. "The bread that I will give for the life of the world is my flesh" (John 6:51). The antidote comes by the same channel through which the poison was delivered—the lips. Have you eaten the bread of life? Have you with faith eaten the Lord's Supper?

Becoming Lavish in Love

Jesus said to Simon, "A creditor had two debtors. One owed five hundred denarii, and the other fifty. Since they could not pay it back, he graciously forgave them both. So, which of them will love him more?" (Luke 7:41–42). A denarius was roughly a day's wage, but the important thing is that one debt was ten times larger than the other. Yet neither debtor could pay it back. Jesus came to announce that humans are debtors to God. Since our first parents, we have chosen to ignore his word and create meaning and life apart from him. But much as we try, we cannot get away from our debt to him. Everything about the futility of what we call "progress"—the vast poverty in a rich earth; the inner turmoil of even the greatest minds—spells our quarrel with our master. The reason the Bible is a story of God's triumph, a story of love and salvation, is that *since we could not pay God back, he graciously provided the means to forgive us.* Jesus, more than announcing our debt, came to pay it with his own blood.

Those who have experienced much forgiveness are free to extend much love. How great do you think is your debt to God? A measure of fifty or five hundred? Like Simon's, is your ability to love cold, frozen by the high altitude from which you look down on everyone else? The only way your heart will melt and become lavish in love, like the heart of the woman who kissed Jesus's feet, is to believe that God in Jesus is extending to you the payment of an astronomical debt you could never repay. All you must do is take and eat.

CHAPTER 3

People

Widespread among Christians today is the belief that I can be a Christian without involvement in the church. In a society where the individual comes before the whole, it is easy to read the Bible as if God were addressing you or me in isolation. To be sure, the pages of the Bible are filled with the personal address of God— not only to Abraham, Moses, David, or Isaiah, but also to you and me. Yet even such intimate, personal prayers as those found in the book of Psalms should be understood as expressions of worship from someone who lived in the midst of the faith *community*.

The mission of Jesus was to save people from their sin and gather them into the family of God, the church. And nowhere is this collective and familial nature of his followers clearer than in the Lord's Prayer (see Matt 6:9–13). The entire prayer references us, the children of God, not me, the isolated self of the twenty-first-century West. We would more naturally say the prayer in this fashion:

> *My* Father in heaven . . .
> Give *me* today *my* daily bread.
> And forgive *me my* debts,
> as *I* also have forgiven *my* debtors.
> And do not bring *me* into temptation,
> but deliver *me* from the evil one.

Such a focus on "me," "my," and "I" makes the sublime words of Jesus almost unrecognizable.

But what do I lose when I read Scripture as an isolated "I," an island unto myself? Moreover, given that I am an individual, living in an individualistic culture, how can I develop a healthy understanding of my relationship with God as part of a larger story that includes many others? These are important questions, and we will attempt to answer them by highlighting the preeminence of "the people of God" in the biblical narrative.

One Man, One Nation, the Whole World

When God confronted Adam and Eve, his judgment began with the serpent. One of the things God says to the serpent is, "I will put hostility between . . . your offspring and [the woman's] offspring" (Gen 3:15). This theme of offspring (or seed) is significant in Scripture, particularly in Genesis. What we learn is that there are two lines that can be traced from Genesis and beyond—one line contends against God, and one line is chosen by God to accomplish his purposes for the earth. Take, for example, Cain and Abel. Cain killed his brother out of envy. But God then gave Seth to Adam and Eve. "Adam was intimate with his wife again, and she gave birth to a son and named him Seth, for she said, 'God has given me another child [lit. "seed"] in place of Abel, since Cain killed him'" (Gen 4:25). Through the line of Seth came Noah, who listened to the voice of God. But even the line of Noah divided again, so that Canaan was opposed to God, but Shem carried the seed through whom Abram (later renamed "Abraham") would come.

> The LORD said to Abram:
> Go out from your land,

your relatives, and your father's house
to the land that I will show you.
I will make you into a great nation,
I will bless you,
I will make your name great,
and you will be a blessing.
I will bless those who bless you,
I will curse anyone who treats you with contempt,
and all the peoples on earth will be blessed through you.
(Gen 12:1–3)

Unfortunately, in much American preaching, it is easy to make a passage like this one more about Abraham than about God's purposes. The promises to Abraham are certainly grand, and they came at a cost. He must leave all he knows—his land, his relatives, his father's house. But the direction of the promise moves away from Abraham, or rather *through* Abraham, to everyone with whom he comes in contact. God will bless Abraham, so that he will be a blessing, and all the peoples on earth will be blessed through him (just as curses will fall on those who show contempt for him). Clearly, God is placing Abraham in a special relationship to himself. James 2:23 says that Abraham "was called God's friend." But the larger purpose of this relationship is the formation of a great nation, and even the nation itself has yet a larger role to play by becoming a blessing to all the peoples of the earth. The progression is (1) Abraham, (2) the nation of Israel, (3) the peoples of the world. Our own story, like Abraham's story, must find meaning in the greater story of God as he carries his creation into the new creation.[1]

---

[1] Vaughan Roberts, *God's Big Picture: Tracing the Storyline of the Bible* (Downers Grove, IL: InterVarsity, 2002), gives a short overview of Scripture, keeping in view the larger purposes of God and his kingdom.

By the time Exodus opens, Abraham's family has become a nation, but it is a nation under slavery to Egypt. Like the two debtors in Jesus's parable who could not pay back their debt and needed grace to have it forgiven, Israel, though chosen by God to make him known among the peoples of the earth, also bore the stain of Adam and Eve's disobedience—a debt Israel could not pay. Thus Israel needed grace. Through Moses, God confronted the king of Egypt and snatched his people, Israel, out of the king's clutches. The ten plagues, culminating with the death of the firstborn male of Egypt, human or animal, displayed the power of God. God told the king, "I have let you live for this purpose: to show you my power and to make my name known on the whole earth" (Exod 9:16). Yet Israel was as guilty before God as Egypt, which is why God commanded that the blood of an unblemished, year-old male sheep or goat be put on the doorposts of the Israelites' homes. The blood protected the firstborn of Israel when God's judgment passed over the land. Deliverance came by grace through blood. God's people were now a free nation on their way to their own land.

A Domino Piece in a Colossal Pattern

For people who grew up attending church, certain biblical characters stand out: Noah and the ark; Joseph and his coat of many colors; Moses and the tablets with the Ten Commandments; Joshua and the fallen walls of Jericho; Samson and the pillars of the temple he brought down; David and his sling and stone that killed Goliath; Daniel and the lions' den; Jonah and the fish; and Jesus, of course. Hardly any women make it into this telling of the biblical story. The four Old Testament women featured in Matthew's genealogy of Jesus would be a good place to start (Tamar, Rahab, Ruth, and Bathsheba). But the bigger problem with this big-personality approach to teaching the Bible is that it leaves out more than it includes; it downplays the Bible's main character, God, and his purposes of grace for the world. Instead, it resembles the hero-driven approach to the retelling of, say, American history, which features George Washington, Abraham Lincoln, Henry Ford, and Martin Luther King Jr., to name a few.

History, whether biblical or otherwise, must include the military, political, and other thought leaders that acted as change agents. But, as historians recognize, there are always forces and movements, actions and reactions that sweep over a specific place and time, of which the big personalities are only a domino piece in a colossal pattern. This understanding of history is nowhere more important than in biblical history, where God is not only the first cause but also the guiding hand that initiates, develops, halts, alters, and brings to completion whatever his own counsel has foreordained.

I am not making a point against the virtue of the great heroes and heroines who are familiar to us through Scripture. The entire chapter of Hebrews 11 is built around this premise. But, as Hebrews 11 also reminds us, it is the promise of God that captured their hearts; it is the promise of God that all the people of God—in the past and present, across cultures and centuries—run toward with perseverance (Heb 11:39–12:1). The task for those of us steeped in individualism is to learn to read Scripture and understand our lives as part of a larger vision—God's vision. A domino piece in a colossal pattern.

On God's Covenants with His People

So Abraham became the father of the Israelite nation, and Moses led the nation out of Egypt. At each of these key nation-forming moments, God enacted a *covenant* with his would-be people. A covenant is a solemn oath between two or more parties that binds them in special privileges and responsibilities. A divine covenant binds God to his people under solemn oath to bring about certain promises, and it places obligations on either one or both parties to the covenant.

For instance, God's covenant with Abraham received greater definition as God revealed more of his purposes and promises to him (key passages: Genesis 12, 15, 17, and 22). In Genesis 12, God promised to make Abraham into a great nation and a blessing to the peoples of the earth. In Genesis 15, God promised to give to Abraham's offspring the land of Canaan. "On that day the LORD made a covenant with Abram, saying, 'I give this land to your offspring, from the brook of Egypt to the great river, the Euphrates River'" (v. 18). Further, on that day, God instructed Abraham to bring a number of animals for sacrifice. In Genesis 17, the covenant is given its greatest definition, so it is appropriate to quote the main text in full.

> When Abram was ninety-nine years old, the LORD appeared to him, saying, "I am God Almighty. Live in my presence and be blameless. I will set up my covenant between me and you, and I will multiply you greatly."
>
> Then Abram fell facedown and God spoke with him: "As for me, here is my covenant with you: You will become the father of many nations. Your name will no longer be Abram; your name will be Abraham, for I will make you the father of many nations. I will make you extremely fruitful and will make nations and kings come from you. I will confirm my covenant that is between me and you and your future offspring throughout their generations. It is a permanent covenant to be your God and the God of your offspring after you. And to you and your

future offspring I will give the land where you are resid-
ing—all the land of Canaan—as a permanent possession,
and I will be their God." (vv. 1–8)

God claimed Abraham as his own. Because of who God is ("I am
God Almighty"), Abraham was to "live in [God's] presence and
be blameless." God then set his covenant with Abraham and made
important promises: (1) to make him the father of many nations;
God changed Abram's name, which meant "exalted father," to Abraham, which means "father of a multitude," because many nations
and kings will come from him; (2) to confirm the covenant with
Abraham's future offspring ("it is a permanent covenant"), specifically, to be their God; (3) to give his future offspring the land of
Canaan as a permanent possession. Then God gave Abraham the
sign of the covenant: circumcision. "Every one of your males must
be circumcised. You must circumcise the flesh of your foreskin to
serve as a sign of the covenant between me and you" (vv. 10–11).
Circumcision was the sign that showed that a descendant of Abraham had received God's covenant.

It must be noted that when God made the covenant with Abraham, to make him "father of a multitude," Abraham was 100 years
old. His wife Sarah was 90 years old and barren, and they had no
children together. So when God told him this, Abraham did what
you and I would have done: he laughed (v. 17). Yet, when the book
of Exodus opens, Abraham's descendants have become a nation.
God had been faithful to his promises.

After liberating them from Egypt, God also made a covenant
with the nation of Israel. "Now if you will carefully listen to me
and keep my covenant, you will be my own possession out of all
the peoples, although the whole earth is mine, and you will be my
kingdom of priests and my holy nation" (Exod 19:5–6). God then

gave Israel the stipulations of the covenant, which included the Ten Commandments, one of which was to observe the seventh day as a Sabbath, a day of rest and a sign of the covenant. Additionally, God instituted the animal sacrificial system, spelled out in parts of Exodus and Leviticus, through which a people who bore the stain of Adam and Eve's sin could be in relationship to a holy God. "Without the shedding of blood there is no forgiveness" (Heb 9:22).

Another important covenant takes place a few hundred years after God made his covenant with Israel. From within the nation of Israel, God chose David as the one through whom the promises made earlier to Abraham would come to greatest fulfillment. God said to David (through the prophet Nathan),

> The LORD declares to you: The LORD himself will make a house for you. When your time comes and you rest with your fathers, I will raise up after you your descendant, who will come from your body, and I will establish his kingdom. He is the one who will build a house for my name, and I will establish the throne of his kingdom forever. I will be his father, and he will be my son. When he does wrong, I will discipline him with a rod of men and blows from mortals. But my faithful love will never leave him as it did when I removed it from Saul, whom I removed from before you. Your house and kingdom will endure before me forever, and your throne will be established forever. (2 Sam 7:11–16)

David the king had wanted to build a house for God, a temple, but God said that he would build a house for David, a dynasty. Parts of this promise were fulfilled in David's son, Solomon, but the ultimate fulfillment was reserved for David's ultimate descendant,

Jesus Christ, whose kingdom would endure forever. At each stage, the covenant with Abraham received greater definition.[2]

The Tension of Rebellion

For our purposes, it is important to note that from the time of Adam and Eve's sin against God, God endeavored to make himself known; he pledged himself in covenant—with Abraham, with Israel, with David—to do good to those who kept his covenant. He promised never to withdraw his faithful love. To be sure, the line from God's promises to fulfillment was hardly straight. As you read the Old Testament, a constant theme stands out: rebellion. People stayed together when God said "disperse" (Genesis 11). Israel built a golden calf when God said not to worship by means of an image (Exodus 32). They refused to take on Canaan when God said to conquer (Numbers 13–14). Their hands were covered with bloodshed when God asked them to do good, pursue justice, defend the rights of the fatherless, and plead the widow's cause (Isaiah 1).

Starting with Adam and Eve's rebellion, the human race has believed that autonomy from God leads to flourishing and self-fulfillment when, in fact, it brings ruin and incurs judgment. At one point, similar to the banishment of Adam and Eve from the garden of Eden, God exiled Israel away from the land of promise. It appears that God had rescinded the covenant as he sent a message to the whole nation through the prophet Hosea regarding the name to be given to one of Hosea's sons. God said, "Name him Lo-ammi, for you are not my people, and I will not be your God" (Hos 1:9). The

---

[2]   For more on God's covenants, see O. Palmer Robertson, *The Christ of the Covenants* (Phillipsburg, NJ: P&R, 1980); Peter J. Gentry and Stephen J. Wellum, *Kingdom through Covenant: A Biblical Theological Understanding of the Covenants* (Wheaton, IL: Crossway, 2012).

Hebrew name *Lo-ammi* means "not my people." Israel through its behavior persisted in unfaithfulness to God to the point that God no longer wanted to be identified as Israel's God; he certainly did not want them to be his people. And yet, not even the awful behavior of his people could cause God to withdraw his faithful love, for also through Hosea God promised that forgiveness was coming. He promised that he would say to Lo-ammi: "You are my people," and Israel would respond: "You are my God" (Hos 2:23).

How would this constant move toward rebellion be transformed into the people delighting in their God?

God Loves and Wounds

There are many sentiments about Jesus in our cultural air, none more popular than *Jesus loves me.* But those who have actually encountered Jesus as presented in the Gospels and John's Revelation know that to take him at his word can feel more like hitting a concrete wall at sixty-five miles per hour. At Epcot, in Disney World, there is a ride called Test Track that showcases how automakers make cars. The ride ends with the car you're in accelerating to sixty-five miles an hour moving toward a barrier, a solid wall. At the very last minute, the barrier flies open like a door, and the car exits onto a racetrack. It's quite the thrill. In a similar way, on the other side of hitting the wall that is Jesus we find life—life on his terms. Yes, *God loves me,* but he also wounds me. "He wounds but he also bandages; he strikes, but his hands also heal" (Job 5:18).

We hit a wall when the popular concept that Jesus came to be in relationship with "me" (understood in isolation from his people) meets the words of Jesus that say, "*Our* Father in heaven." That pronoun, that first-person plural possessive, contains both the strike and the healing hand. In fact, the nine first-person pronouns in the prayer of Matthew 6:9–13 are all plural (italics added).

> *Our* Father in heaven,
> your name be honored as holy.
> Your kingdom come.
> Your will be done
> on earth as it is in heaven.
> Give *us* today *our* daily bread.
> And forgive *us our* debts,
> As *we* also have forgiven *our* debtors.
> And do not bring *us* into temptation,
> but deliver *us* from the evil one.

His words wound because I have been inappropriately conditioned, both culturally and by my own heart, to believe that unless I follow my deepest desires I will never find happiness. The self, my self, is supreme. But his words also heal because even as they wound they invite. They invite me to see that there is another name that is far greater than mine, and there is another family—to which I belong but of which I am only a part—that is the heir to this enduring prayer. The prayer Jesus puts on our lips reorients our sense of identity. I want to discover who I am in light of who God is; who I am in light of the family of God to which I belong. What we call the Lord's Prayer—infinite in scope even as it fits in one tweet—should really be called the Prayer of God's Family.

Our Father in Heaven

As I talk to Christians, I realize that a major challenge of our living in a postmodern, post-Christian world is dialoguing with people who don't share a Christian worldview. Whatever the issue—abortion, gender, marriage, parental authority—relating to someone who doesn't hold Christian beliefs feels increasingly difficult. The difference in perspective boils down to those four words in the first line of the Lord's Prayer: *Our Father in heaven.*

Although many worldviews emerge in our contemporary world, two of them dominate Western culture. We come up against them just about every day. One says, we are here as the chance result of nonliving chemicals. The other says, we are here as the loving creation of our Father in heaven. This is the dividing line. Secular thought sees the world as ultimately *impersonal.* There is no mind, design, or grand purpose in the universe. The Christian worldview sees the world as ultimately *personal.* There is design and purpose in the universe because of our Father in heaven.

On an impersonal view of the universe, a number of philosophers and scholars have cogently argued, we struggle to explain basic and important human features such as meaning, morality, reason, and love.[3] However, if the universe is ultimately personal, then these human features make sense. This conceptualization of God as our heavenly Father was one of Jesus's main points in teaching, especially in the Sermon on the Mount. Let us take a short sample.

He began with the Beatitudes (Matt 5:3–10), where he called his followers to be poor in spirit, mournful, meek, hungry and thirsty for righteousness, merciful, pure in heart, and peacemakers. Such

---

[3]   See, e.g., Alasdair MacIntyre, *After Virtue*, 3rd ed. (Notre Dame, IN: University of Notre Dame Press, 1981), and *Whose Justice? Which Rationality?* (Notre Dame, IN: University of Notre Dame Press, 1988); Charles Taylor, *A Secular Age* (Cambridge, MA: Belknap, Harvard University Press, 2007); Alvin Plantinga, *Where the Conflict Really Lies: Science, Religion, and Naturalism* (Oxford: Oxford University Press, 2011); C. S. Lewis, *Mere Christianity* (New York: Macmillan, 1952); Rebecca McLaughlin, *Confronting Christianity: 12 Hard Questions for the World's Largest Religion* (Wheaton: Crossway, 2019).

people are the salt of the earth and the light of the world, those who must let their light shine before others, "so that they may see your good works and give glory to your Father in heaven" (v. 16). Our motivation for doing good things should be that others might think highly of God our Father, not us. That's what "give glory" means.

Then Jesus spoke of the greater righteousness of the kingdom, which is a righteousness of the heart, not of the externals of religion.[4] He gave six examples of areas that need our attention: the seriousness of anger and lust, the hardness of heart expressed in divorce, the lack of truthfulness expressed in the practice of taking oaths, the instinct to seek revenge, and the tribal nature of our love (vv. 21–48). He concluded that section by saying, "But I tell you, love your enemies and pray for those who persecute you, so that you may be children of your Father in heaven. For he causes his sun to rise on the evil and the good, and sends rain on the righteous and the unrighteous" (vv. 44–45). The generous spirit of our Father in heaven should kill our tribal love and make us equally liberal in our expression of love for all, including those outside our group.

One final example from the Sermon on the Mount comes when Jesus emphasized the human thirst to perform and be seen by others. He contrasted an empty form of religion whose goal is to receive human praise with the greater righteousness of God's kingdom in which followers of Jesus were content to be seen and praised by their Father in heaven "who sees in secret." When giving, he said, do not sound a trumpet. When praying, do not stand on street corners to be seen by people. When fasting, do not make it obvious to people.

---

[4]   R. T. France, *The Gospel of Matthew,* NICNT (Grand Rapids: Eerdmans, 2007), 190, says, "Those who are to belong to God's new realm must move beyond literal observance of rules, however good and scriptural, to a new consciousness of what it means to please God, one which penetrates beneath the surface level of rules to be obeyed to a more radical openness of knowing and doing the underlying will of 'your Father in heaven.'"

Instead, do all these things in private. And he repeated essentially the same statement three times, "And your Father who sees in secret will reward you" (Matt 6:4, 6, 18). Jesus frees us from our need to be seen by others because we have a Father in heaven who sees us in secret and rewards us. We do not have to put on a show. The approval we're after comes from God. It's not wrong to want to be seen, but it is wrong, and utterly unsatisfying, to want to be seen by people.

Taken together, in just these three sections alone, Jesus put forth an expansive view of God that tears down and rebuilds the self's identity around the knowledge and experience of God as our Father. We begin to do good in the world from an inner motivation that shifts away from self-glory to the glory of our Father in heaven. We strive to replace our selfish tendency to prefer our own group and exclude or demonize those whose ideologies oppose our own with an ethic of love and a spirit of understanding. Why? Because our Father is kind even to the evil and the unjust. We end the brutal quest for the approval of others because we know our Father sees us and rewards us, and no other vision or voice bestows more value upon us. The self that emerges possesses more humility, magnanimity, and confidence. People with such inner strength of character open themselves up to others with trust and delight, not least because they understand that God is not just "my Father" but "our Father in heaven."[5]

We Follow and Grow—Together

Mark in his Gospel records an episode when Jesus's family did not approve of his actions. Jesus was teaching in a house, and they came

---

[5] For an insightful exposition of the Sermon on the Mount, see Jonathan T. Pennington, *The Sermon on the Mount and Human Flourishing: A Theological Commentary* (Grand Rapids: Baker Academic, 2017).

out to restrain him. In the same episode, a number of scribes from Jerusalem also took issue with the ministry of Jesus. They attributed his exorcisms to an evil spirit. The episode turns on Jesus's reply to those who announced to him that his family was waiting outside the house for him. Mark writes, "He replied to them, 'Who are my mother and my brothers?' Looking at those sitting in a circle around him, he said, 'Here are my mother and my brothers! Whoever does the will of God is my brother and sister and mother'" (Mark 3:33–35).

In America, the nuclear family is a cornerstone of society. People today debate what constitutes a family, but its importance is not up for debate. Families are featured in advertisements for home mortgages, insurance, hot dogs, vacations, cars, colleges, clothes, entertainment, and much more. Everyone smiles in these photographs and videos as they enjoy the comfort, relationship, and ease of family. This happy family portrait encounters a wall when Jesus answers his own family members with what can be understood only as a slight: "Whoever does the will of God is my brother and sister and mother." Remember: his birth mother and blood brothers were waiting outside.

Think about this. Our individualistic ethos does not isolate the self completely. It makes room for one's family of origin, and even more so, one's family of choice or procreation. Yet Jesus reconfigures family boundary lines around those who do the will of God, here identified as those "sitting in a circle around him," listening to his words.

That picture—sitting around Jesus, listening to his words—captures the essence of the family of God. Elsewhere in the New Testament, when Jesus speaks with the rich ruler who wants to know how to inherit eternal life, Jesus tells him to obey the commandments. What's so curious is that Jesus speaks only of the six commandments that address our obligation to our fellow human beings (Mark 10:19).[6] For the longest time I have wondered, Why did Jesus not bring up the first table of the commandments, the ones referring to our obligation to God? But now I realize that he did. After the man said he had kept all the commandments, this is what Jesus said to him: "Go, sell all you have and give to the poor, and you will have treasure in heaven. Then come, follow me" (Mark 10:21). There it is. Jesus said, "Follow me." When we follow Jesus, we are obeying the first four commandments, the ones that address our obligation to God, because God himself said on the Mount of Transfiguration, "This is my beloved son; listen to him!" (Mark 9:7). The rich man wanted something to do in order to inherit eternal life. He wanted an *action*. But what he needed—what we all need—is a *person*, Jesus Christ. Sadly, the man was unwilling to follow him. Before Jesus asked the man to follow him, Mark tells us the following, "Looking at him, Jesus loved him" (Mark 10:21). Jesus *loved* him even as he wounded him. The first commandment ("Do not have other gods besides me," Exod 20:3) and Jesus saying "follow me" are one and the same.

This act of following Jesus, which we will tease out more fully in the chapter titled "Yoke," is something we do *together*. His family comprises "those sitting around him." It takes the family of God gathering together to listen to Jesus's words for each one of us to grasp fully the love of God in Christ. This is one of Paul's great insights in his prayer that connects the togetherness of God's people with our ability to comprehend God's vast love for us. He says, "I pray that you, being rooted and firmly established in love, may be able to comprehend *with all the saints* what is the length and width, height and depth of God's love, and to know Christ's love that

---

[6] The first four commandments in Exodus 20 address our obligation to God; the last six deal with our obligation to our neighbor.

surpasses knowledge, so that you may be filled with all the fullness of God" (Eph 3:17–19, italics added). No one can by him- or herself see and enjoy the length, width, height, and depth of God's love. We each are too small, in thought, feeling, or action, to absorb and be transformed by God's infinite wisdom and love. Our finitude is a prison, and the key to unlock it is the company of *all the saints*, the people of God. Whether it is a bleary-eyed nursing mother or a teen-ager whose testimony at baptism describes his passage from only fearing God to actually loving him or a couple in their eighties that walks into church, hand-in-hand every week, after many decades, to hear God's Word; whether it is a cancer survivor or an immigrant who came to America for the American Dream only to have God expand her dream beyond what she could have ever imagined or simply someone mourning one of the dozens of losses that life deals to us—we come to know God in all his wisdom, faithfulness, and love as we come to know God's people and see his love reflected in those sitting around him, listening to his words.[7]

Rebellion Turns into Delight

In the opening chapter of Matthew's Gospel, the angel who announces to Joseph that Mary is with child from the Holy Spirit says to him, "She will give birth to a son, and you are to name him Jesus, because he will save his people from their sins" (v. 21). The mission of Jesus was to bring salvation to his *people*, specifically salvation from their sins. As Matthew tells the story, Jesus went about teaching, doing

---

[7]   On the importance of the church for the Christian life, see Joseph H. Heller-man, *When the Church Was a Family: Recapturing Jesus' Vision for Authentic Christian Community* (Nashville: B&H, 2009); Hellerman, *Why We Need the Church to Become More like Jesus* (Eugene, OR: Cascade, 2017); Dietrich Bonhoeffer, *Life Together* (New York: Harper & Row, 1954).

works of power, and healing. His healing powers were a physical, verifiable way of demonstrating that he also could cure the soul. The connection was present in the writings of the prophet Isaiah, who had said, "He himself took our weaknesses and carried our diseases" (Matt 8:17, quoting Isa 53:4).[8] What is fascinating is the very next verse in Isaiah: "But he was pierced because of our rebellion, crushed because of our iniquities; punishment for our peace was on him, and we are healed by his wounds" (v. 5). Jesus carried our diseases and was crushed for our iniquities.

Aware that his mission to save his people from their sins was reaching its culmination, Jesus prepared his disciples on the night when he was betrayed, the night before his death.

> As they were eating, Jesus took bread, blessed and broke it, gave it to the disciples, and said, "Take and eat it; this is my body." Then he took a cup, and after giving thanks, he gave it to them and said, "Drink from it, all of you. For this is my blood of the covenant, which is poured out for many for the forgiveness of sins." (Matt 26:26–28)

The "blood of the covenant." God had made covenants with Abraham, with Israel, and with David, each with different particulars, but all with the same intent—to bless all the families of the earth through the offspring of Abraham. Yet, as discussed above, God's people (not to mention the rest of the world's inhabitants) had a constant bent toward rebellion. Only when the Son of God came and was pierced for our rebellion could the hearts of God's people be finally healed. Only then would their rebellion turn into delight in God. This is the power of the new covenant, which is made effectual

---

[8] In Matt 9:1–8, Jesus brings together his ability both to forgive sin and to heal physical illness.

by the death of Jesus Christ. Deliverance came by grace through blood.

We must remember that the institution of the Lord's Supper was not given to Peter or James or John. Jesus gave the bread and the cup to the apostles *as a group*, the ones who just a few weeks later would launch the church in the power of God's Spirit. The new covenant belongs to the church. It is the covenant of those who call God "our Father in heaven."

Fish out of Water

My hope is that this brief survey of the important theme of God's people in Scripture would heighten our love for the church. We will explore key aspects of the church and its mission in the next chapters; for now, it should be obvious why the Western tendency to read Scripture in isolation and live the Christian life cut off from the family of God is an anomaly. Fish out of water die, and Christians out of the church never mature. We need to grasp the length, width, height and depth of God's love *together with all the saints*. My relationship with God is personal but not private. It's a relationship that is a part of a larger story, a domino piece in a colossal pattern, and those who know Jesus by faith delight to join hands with Jesus's spiritual mothers, brothers, and sisters so that they can listen to his words.

CHAPTER 4

Presence

O ne of the most memorable stories in the Gospels is the story of the storm. Matthew, Mark, and Luke narrate it, but Mark gives the fullest version. Jesus wanted to go beyond traditional limits, into unclean territory. To do so, he had to cross the Sea of Galilee, which was subject to furious squalls. It was nighttime and, sure enough, a great windstorm arose and water began to fill the boat. But Jesus was sleeping. Now, the disciples did what you and I would've done: they awoke the master. And, as Mark narrates it, they were even harsh with him. They said, "Teacher! Don't you care that we're going to die?" Jesus got up, rebuked the wind, and said to the chaotic sea, "Silence! Be still!" Then, Mark writes, "The wind ceased, and there was a great calm" (Mark 4:39).

There is an element in this story with which we readily connect: the storm. We talk about our lives using the metaphor of a storm. *This storm shall pass.* A major illness, a trial in marriage, financial pressures, a tantrum-prone child, a bruised friendship, political upheaval, a deadly virus. We refer to all these things as storms, and there is something deeply comforting about the fact that Jesus made the storm stop. "The wind ceased, and there was a great calm." In fact, in some segments of the Christian church, the message boils down to this: *Come to Jesus, and the storms of your life will be over.*

But if we read the story carefully, we realize that the story does not end with "a great calm." It ends with a great fear and a great question. There is a reversal. At first, the winds and sea were agitated; at the end, the sea was calm but the disciples were agitated. The stillness of the sea contrasts with the disturbance in the disciples' hearts. The storm made the disciples despair of their lives, but the authority of Jesus over wind and sea made them "amazed" (Matt 8:27), "terrified" (Mark 4:41), and "fearful and amazed" (Luke 8:25).

The question Jesus asked the disciples in the story puzzles me every time I read it. He said, "Why are you afraid? Do you still have no faith?" (Mark 4:40). The disciples interpreted Jesus's sleep as a lack of care. Not so. They also thought they were about to die. Wrong again. Jesus considered inappropriate what to us seems like a very sensible response—fear in the face of a furious storm. But what they were missing all along was an understanding of who was on the boat with them, which is why the episode closes with a great question, a question that indeed carries forward the narrative of every Gospel account, "Who then is this? Even the wind and the sea obey him!" (v. 41).

In the course of forty-eight hours, significant events took place in my local congregation. A couple had a baby, a moment of both rejoicing and sheer exhaustion for the mother. Another couple's baby was hospitalized for surgery because she had holes in her heart (holes bigger than the doctors had anticipated). A wife found her husband on the kitchen floor having seizures (the first but not the last time this happened). Someone else had to go in for a biopsy. Another parent won full custody of his child. For each person, fear clung closely in these "storms." Yet there is a deeper experience for the person of faith, especially in the midst of such storms—that is, the presence of God, which is our theme in this chapter.

A Man Speaks with His Friend

Not long after the formation of Israel as a nation, the people quickly broke faith with God. They built a statue, a golden calf, and worshiped by means of it. This event put on display the people's innate disposition to resist the word of God—what God in Exodus called their "stiff-necked" nature—for God's word had already come to them with the instruction, "Do not make an idol for yourself, whether in the shape of anything in the heavens above or on the earth below or in the waters under the earth. Do not bow in worship to them, and do not serve them" (Exod 20:4–5).

But in spite of their rebellion, God kept his promise to Abraham to lead the people to the land of Canaan, though he told Moses that he, God, would not go with them. "Go up to a land flowing with milk and honey. But I will not go up with you because you are a stiff-necked people; otherwise, I might destroy you on the way" (Exod 33:3). Moses, however, was less interested in the promise than in God's presence. The withdrawal of God's presence was too much for him to bear, so he demanded to know whom God was sending with him and the people. In an incredible turn, God replies to Moses: "My presence will go with you, and I will give you rest" (v. 14). But Moses, as if he had not heard God, retorted, "If your presence does not go, don't make us go up from here" (v. 15). Moses went on to explain that the only thing that distinguished Israel from all the people of the earth was the presence of God in their midst.

As the narrative develops, it seems that every time Moses made a request, God conceded, only to have Moses ratchet up his next request. After God said, "I will do this very thing you have asked,"— that is, send his presence with Israel—Moses asked, "Please, let me see your glory" (vv. 17–18). The reader gets the feeling that God is not put off by Moses's boldness and persistence, but, on the contrary, endeared to him. This exchange is perhaps a window into God's relationship with Moses, described verses earlier as, "The LORD would speak with Moses face to face, just as a man speaks with his friend" (v. 11).

"Please, let me see your glory" was Moses's request. God then said, "I will cause all my goodness to pass in front of you, and I will proclaim the name 'the LORD' before you. I will be gracious to whom I will be gracious, and I will have compassion on whom I will have compassion" (v. 19). God came down, proclaimed his name before Moses, and made a covenant with him and with Israel. Striking in the narration is Moses's concern for God's presence and God's desire, in response to Moses's requests, to draw near to Moses and make himself known in all his goodness.

It was not the land of promise or the size of the nation that mattered to Moses. It was the favor of God, expressed in his presence with his people as they journeyed. "How will it be known that I and your people have found favor with you unless you go with us?" (v. 16).[1]

The Presence of God with Israel

As we saw in a previous chapter, when Adam and Eve rebelled against God, they were cast out of the garden of Eden, away from the presence of God. But rather than leaving humanity in darkness and ignorant of the greatest reality in the universe, God made himself known in the world by entering into a special relationship, a covenant, with Israel. This relationship was sustained by God's

---

[1]   Peter Enns, *Exodus,* The NIV Application Commentary (Grand Rapids: Zondervan, 2000), 581, emphasizes that the issue in Exodus 33 is that God is willing to go with Moses but not with the people as a result of their rebellion. Hence, Moses pleads "unless you go with *us.*"

word, which is why God gave Moses his law, and Moses had to be careful to do everything according to God's word.

Of chief importance in the life of Israel was the question of worship. How could a rebellious, unholy people be in the presence of a holy God? So much of God's instruction to Israel, as we see in the Pentateuch (the first five books of the Old Testament), is concerned with this subject. God gave Israel priests who came from a specific tribe (Levi) and had to purify themselves before they could intercede before God on behalf of the people. He also instituted the sacrificial system, by which animals were offered for the sins of the people, but it could not be just any animal; the animals had to meet God's specifications. Finally, God gave instructions on the tabernacle, the tent that housed the ark containing the tablets with the commandments, and the courtyard where the sacrifices were offered. You can read the specifics of these instructions and events in the second half of Exodus. The book culminates with a summary of what made Israel a nation like no other in the world.

> So Moses finished the work.
>
> The cloud covered the tent of meeting, and the glory of the LORD filled the tabernacle. Moses was unable to enter the tent of meeting because the cloud rested on it, and the glory of the LORD filled the tabernacle.
>
> The Israelites set out whenever the cloud was taken up from the tabernacle throughout all the stages of their journey. If the cloud was not taken up, they did not set out until the day it was taken up. For the cloud of the LORD was over the tabernacle by day, and there was a fire inside the cloud by night, visible to the entire house of Israel throughout all the stages of their journey. (Exod 40:33–38)

The glory of God filled the tabernacle—in a cloud by day, as a fire by night. Only when the cloud moved did the people move. The presence of God was guiding his people through every stage of their journey.

A few centuries later when Solomon builds the temple, the more permanent form of the tabernacle, a similar event took place. "When the priests came out of the holy place, the cloud filled the LORD's temple, and because of the cloud, the priests were not able to continue ministering, for the glory of the LORD filled the temple" (1 Kgs 8:10–11). These two events—the completion of the tabernacle by Moses and of the temple by Solomon—were high-water marks in the life of Israel, not because of the human achievement they represented, but because of God's response in sending his glory, his presence, causing his goodness, to rest among his people.

In his prayer of dedication of the temple, Solomon recognized the unique privilege of having Israel's God dwell in their midst. The temple was the place about which God had said, "My name will be there" (1 Kgs 8:29; see Deut 12:11). Time and again in the prayer (1 Kings 8) Solomon connected the temple and the name of God. For example,

> When your people Israel are defeated before an enemy,
> because they have sinned against you,
> and they return to you and praise your name,
> and they pray and plead with you
> for mercy in this temple . . . (v. 33)

> When the skies are shut and there is no rain,
> because they have sinned against you,
> and they pray toward this place
> and praise your name . . . (v. 35)

Even for the foreigner who is not of your people Israel
but has come from a distant land
because of your name—
for they will hear of your great name,
strong hand, and outstretched arm,
and will come and pray toward this temple . . . (vv. 41–42)

When your people go out to fight against their enemies,
wherever you send them,
and they pray to the LORD
in the direction of the city you have chosen
and the temple I have built for your name . . . (v. 44)

Solomon believed that Israel would flourish and recover from defeat or famine due to sin when they addressed God in the direction of the temple, the place where God's named dwelled. Even peoples from other lands would be attracted to Israel's God and come and praise his name in the temple.

At the same time, Solomon noted that the Creator of the universe could not be contained by such a small structure. "But will God indeed live on earth? Even heaven, the highest heaven, cannot contain you, much less this temple I have built" (v. 27). A tension, then, emerges. The proper dwelling place of God is heaven, though even the heavens are too small for him; at the same time, God chose Jerusalem, and in Jerusalem he chose the temple as the place on earth where his name would reside. (Remember that when Moses asked God to show him his glory, God proclaimed his name, "the LORD," over him.) The temple in localized form contained the name of God, which not even the highest heavens can contain. And where his name is, there God is.

Yet Israel was holding fire. God heard Solomon's prayer and accepted it, but he also warned Solomon:

> If you or your sons turn away from following me and do not keep my commands—my statutes that I have set before you—and if you go and serve other gods and bow in worship to them, I will cut off Israel from the land I gave them, and I will reject the temple I have sanctified for my name. Israel will become an object of scorn and ridicule among all the peoples. (1 Kgs 9:6–7)

This warning indeed became reality, as a cursory reading of 1–2 Kings and the Prophets makes clear. The people's disobedience to God led to the loss of the land, the temple, and the presence of God. The prophet Ezekiel even saw a vision of the glory of God leaving the city. "The glory of the LORD rose up from within the city and stopped on the mountain east of the city" (Ezek 11:23). Even when the exiles returned to the land of Judah, after seventy years of exile, there is no narrated episode of God's glory returning and his presence filling the temple. The one thing Moses asked for, the one thing that made Israel unique among the nations—the presence of God—had departed from his people. God would remain faithful to his covenant promises, but in real and painful ways for the people of God after the exile, the favor, peace, and prosperity associated with God's presence paled in comparison to the prophets' vision. For example, Isa 60:1–3 says: "Arise, shine, for your light has come, and the glory of the LORD shines over you. For look, darkness will cover the earth, and total darkness the peoples; but the LORD will shine over you, and his glory will appear over you. Nations will come to your light, and kings to your shining brightness." Israel after exile was no light to the nations.

God with Us

Students of Matthew's Gospel know that Matthew highlights the theme of God's presence among his people, both in the opening and closing chapters of his Gospel.

> See, the virgin will become pregnant
> and give birth to a son,
> and they will name him Immanuel,
> which is translated "God is with us." (Matt 1:23)

> Jesus came near and said to them, "All authority has been given to me in heaven and on earth. Go, therefore, and make disciples of all nations, baptizing them in the name of the Father and of the Son and of the Holy Spirit, teaching them to observe everything I have commanded you. And remember, I am with you always, to the end of the age." (Matt 28:18–20)

Near the middle of his Gospel, Matthew has placed another important statement about the with-us-ness of Jesus, his attribute of being *with us*. Jesus said,

> Again, truly I tell you, if two of you on earth agree about any matter that you pray for, it will be done for you by my Father in heaven. For where two or three are gathered together in my name, I am there among them. (Matt 18:19–20)

In these statements, we learn that one of the names for Jesus is *Immanuel*, a Hebrew word that Matthew translates for his audience:

God is with us.[2] We also learn that when two or three of Jesus's disciples gather *in his name*, his presence is among them. So rather than having to pray toward the temple, where God's name dwelt, as in the days of Solomon, praying in the name of Jesus mediates the presence of the One who is "God with us" to the followers of Jesus.

Furthermore, the name of God the Father—the name that in the Old Testament God proclaimed over his people as a demonstration of his presence among them—also includes the Son and the Holy Spirit. Jesus says to baptize his disciples, not in the "names" (plural), but in the "name" (singular) of the Father, Son, and Holy Spirit. *One name. Three persons.* The divine name includes Father, Son, and Holy Spirit. Christians accustomed to hearing about the Trinity may find little novelty in this statement. Yet, for any devout Jewish person in the first century who believed that God is one and there is no other, to make such a claim was nothing short of amazing.

Here Is Your God

Let's reflect on some of the ways Matthew developed this theme of God's presence among his people in the coming of Jesus.

In the ministry of John the Baptist, one Scripture more than any other seems to have defined his prophetic role: "A voice of one crying out: Prepare the way of the LORD in the wilderness; make a straight highway for our God in the desert" (Isa 40:3).[3] This Scripture in Isaiah is significant because it opens the section that announces with

---

[2] For a thorough analysis of the theme of divine presence in Matthew, see David D. Kupp, *Matthew's Emmanuel*, SNTSMS (Cambridge: Cambridge University Press, 1996).

[3] Matthew, Mark, and John quote Isa 40:3. Luke quotes Isa 40:3–5. See Matt 3:3; Mark 1:3; Luke 3:4–6; John 1:23.

boundless hope the coming salvation of God, Isaiah 40–55. In Isaiah 40:3, the prophet spoke of a voice crying out, a voice whose role was *preparation*. The one for whom the way was to be prepared was Yahweh, the Lord. The one for whom the highway was to be made straight was God. Then John showed up saying he *is* the voice in the desert (see John 1:23), and the one for whom he prepares the way is Jesus. *When the people expected the coming of Yahweh, our God, John the Baptist pointed them to Jesus.*

Another text in Isaiah speaks of the result of God's coming to his people: the blind will see, the deaf will hear, the lame will walk, and the mute will sing for joy.

> Strengthen the weak hands,
> steady the shaking knees!
> Say to the cowardly: "Be strong; do not fear!
> Here is your God; vengeance is coming.
> God's retribution is coming; he will save you."
> Then the eyes of the blind will be opened,
> and the ears of the deaf unstopped.
> Then the lame will leap like a deer,
> and the tongue of the mute will sing for joy. (Isa 35:3–6)

Like the other evangelists, Matthew records many summaries of Jesus's healings.

> Moving on from there, Jesus passed along the Sea of Galilee. He went up on a mountain and sat there, and large crowds came to him, including the lame, the blind, the crippled, those unable to speak, and many others. They put them at his feet, and he healed them. So the crowd was amazed when they saw those unable to speak talking,

the crippled restored, the lame walking, and the blind
seeing, and they gave glory to the God of Israel. (Matt
15:29–31)

These healings are some of the most well-known accounts in the
Gospels. Readers do not often recognize that in the prophecies of
Isaiah such healings take place *as a result* of the coming of God
to his people. Healing was so prominent in the ministry of Jesus
because he is "God with us." *Be strong; do not fear! Here is your
God.*

We now return to the story of the storm with which we opened
this chapter. The disciples feared for their lives when a storm over-
took their boat. But then Jesus woke up, rebuked the winds and sea,
and there was a great calm. The disciples were afraid and amazed
and asked, "What kind of man is this? Even the winds and the sea
obey him!" (Matt 8:27). Keeping that story in the background, I
want you to read Psalm 107:23–30.

Others went to sea in ships,
conducting trade on the vast water.
They saw the LORD's works,
his wondrous works in the deep.
He spoke and raised a stormy wind
that stirred up the waves of the sea.
Rising up to the sky, sinking down to the depths,
their courage melting away in anguish,
they reeled and staggered like a drunkard,
and all their skill was useless.
Then they cried out to the LORD in their trouble,
and he brought them out of their distress.
He stilled the storm to a whisper,

and the waves of the sea were hushed.
They rejoiced when the waves grew quiet.
Then he guided them to the harbor they longed for.

The experience of these tradesmen described in the psalm, I would imagine, was not uncommon—trouble at sea followed by deliverance, which a faithful Jew would attribute to the hand of the Lord. But when we think of Jesus's disciples on the boat in light of Psalm 107, the account becomes chilling. In the psalm, the tradesmen cry out to the Lord, Yahweh. In the Gospel, the disciples cry out to Jesus, a man sleeping next to them. And Jesus, like Yahweh, stilled the storm and the waves. It is hard to imagine anything more bewildering than what the disciples witnessed just then. *A man on a boat spoke to wind and sea, and they obeyed him*! Rather than rejoicing, as the tradesmen in the psalm do following the deliverance, the disciples are amazed and afraid. The storm at this point becomes a thing of the past but also, comparatively speaking, highly inconsequential. A bigger storm is at their side on the boat. What captures the disciples' attention and awe is the presence of Jesus and questions about his identity. "Who then is this? Even the wind and the sea obey him!" (Mark 4:41). Jesus does what only the Lord Yahweh did.[4]

The Triumph of Life

The coming of Jesus to earth was the coming of God to his people. He came not only to bear our sins, but also to be among us.

---

[4] A number of scholars have written on the important theme of the identity of Jesus as the God of Israel: Richard Bauckham, *Jesus and the God of Israel: God Crucified and Other Studies on the New Testament's Christology of Divine Identity* (Grand Rapids: Eerdmans, 2008); Larry W. Hurtado, *Lord Jesus Christ: Devotion to*

In the Gospels, we have a sustained picture of what God dwelling with his people looks like. The poor have an advocate, and food is abundant. Women receive dignity, not for their sexual appeal, but for their rightful place as daughters of the king. The sick are healed. Children are welcomed and esteemed in God's kingdom. Oppressors and abusers of power are not demonized but meet correction and are given an opportunity to turn from their destructive ways. Wisdom flows from Jesus's mouth like water on dry land. Jesus touches people who are defiled without becoming defiled himself. Divine strength meets the opposition of demons, of false teachers, of corrupt politicians, of misguided crowds, and it prevails by yielding to death—even death on a cross. And death itself dies, for three days later, the resurrection of Jesus becomes a foretaste of the triumph of life for all who align themselves with him.

At the very end of Scripture, the book of Revelation gives us a short but unforgettable vision of the return of Christ and the new heaven and new earth. "Then I heard a loud voice from the throne: Look, God's dwelling is with humanity, and he will live with them. They will be his peoples, and God himself will be with them and will be their God" (Rev 21:3). The Gospels have given us a taste of the dwelling of God with humanity. But next time, in the future, there will be no traces of evil, sin, or death. All the political, social, and economic systems of God's new world will produce only harmony, health, and true worship; relationships will be wholesome and life-giving.

Between the presence of God in the coming of Jesus and the presence of God at the renewal of all things, God has not abandoned

---

Jesus in Earliest Christianity (Grand Rapids: Eerdmans, 2003); N. T. Wright, *Jesus and the Victory of God* (Minneapolis: Fortress, 1996), 613–53; Christopher J. H. Wright, *Knowing Jesus through the Old Testament,* 2nd ed. (Downers Grove, IL: IVP Academic, 2014), 252–79.

his people. On the contrary, he has sent us his Spirit, who is God *within* us. To understand how the Spirit of God transforms and gathers God's people from every corner of the world, we must turn to the next chapter.

The storms of life will one day be over. Until then, knowing who is on the boat with us makes all the difference.

CHAPTER 5

Yoke

J oshua Bell, one of the world's most renowned violinists, stood on a subway station in Washington, D.C., on a cold winter morning in 2007. He began to play his violin while more than a thousand people walked by on their morning commute. Hardly anyone stopped to listen. He played for forty-three minutes and only about seven people stayed for any extended time. Only twenty people gave him tips. He collected $32.17 in that forty-three-minute window. When he finished playing, he took his tips and violin and left, to no applause, no recognition, no fanfare.

Clearly, no one realized what had just happened: Joshua Bell had just spent forty-three minutes playing one of the most intricate pieces known to man on a violin that cost $3.5 million. Two nights before, he'd sold out a theater in Boston at $100 a ticket. It is possible to be in the presence of greatness and be completely oblivious to it.[1]

During his ministry on earth, the greatness and glory of Jesus were not always on display. In fact, only on certain occasions did he reveal his glory, and only a few people realized the implications of

---

[1] See Gene Weingarten, "Pearls before Breakfast," *Washington Post*, April 8, 2007, https://www.washingtonpost.com/lifestyle/magazine/pearls-before-breakfast-can-one-of-the-nations-great-musicians-cut-through-the-fog-of-a-dc-rush-hour-lets-find-out/2014/09/23/8a6d46da-4331-11e4-b47c-f5889e061e5f_story.html.

the things Jesus did and said. Many were completely oblivious to it, having eyes that could not see.

Simon, later given the name Peter by Jesus, saw the greatness of Jesus and followed him. In Luke 5, we read about a time when Jesus was teaching the crowd from Simon's boat by the sea. When he finished teaching, he asked Simon to go out for a catch, but Simon said, "Master, we've worked hard all night long and caught nothing. But if you say so, I'll let down the nets" (v. 5). When he did, they took in such a big catch that they needed the help of another boat, and both boats, now overloaded with fish, began to sink. On seeing this, Simon fell to his knees and said to Jesus, "Go away from me, because I'm a sinful man, Lord!" (v. 8). Jesus did not go away. On the contrary, Simon's journey with Jesus was only beginning. "'Don't be afraid,' Jesus told Simon. 'From now on you will be catching people.' Then they brought the boats to land, left everything, and followed him" (vv. 10–11). In this episode, there is a reaction of fear, an assurance of safety, and a call to mission.

John's vision of the exalted Jesus on the island of Patmos has a similar arc. Notice the many similes John used to describe the impression the glorious Christ made on him.[2]

> Then I turned to see whose voice it was that spoke to me.
> When I turned I saw seven golden lampstands, and among
> the lampstands was one like the Son of Man, dressed
> in a robe and with a golden sash wrapped around his
> chest. The hair of his head was white as wool—white as
> snow—and his eyes like a fiery flame. His feet were like
> fine bronze as it is fired in a furnace, and his voice like the

---

[2]   According to Dictionary.com, a simile is "a figure of speech in which two unlikely things are explicitly compared," as when I say to my wife, "You are like the bright sun on a winter morning." I don't really say that to my wife, but I should!

sound of cascading waters. He had seven stars in his right hand; a sharp double-edged sword came from his mouth, and his face was shining like the sun at full strength. (Rev 1:12–16)

Much could be said about the fearsome splendor of Jesus in this portrayal, but our focus is on John's response. John continued. "When I saw him, I fell at his feet like a dead man. He laid his right hand on me and said, 'Don't be afraid. I am the First and the Last, and the Living One. I was dead, but look—I am alive forever and ever, and I hold the keys of death and Hades. Therefore write what you have seen'" (vv. 17–19). John's response was much like Simon's: he fell at the feet of Jesus in a panic. And Jesus's response to John was similar to his response to Simon: "Don't be afraid." Then he commissioned him to write what he saw and send it to the churches (see Rev 1:11). A reaction of fear is met with an assurance of safety and a call to mission. *Our fear must become love, which must become witness.*

Many people have never experienced God in this way. They have never experienced the balance of fearing him and hearing him say, "Fear not," and then receiving from him a commission to work that wakes them up every day with eternal purpose, inspires them to be excellent in all they do, and sends them with courage and compassion to love people. The reaction Simon and John had to the greatness of Jesus was the right one; it's how every human should respond when in the presence of the divine. Remember, it is possible to be in the presence of greatness and be completely blind to it. But fear turns to love when we learn that in Christ God has come not to destroy us but to save us; that Jesus is as much a Savior as he is Lord of Lords; that his word to us is, "don't be afraid;" and that he makes us witnesses in word and deed to the power of his death and resurrection. Our fear must become love, which must become witness.

However, becoming witnesses in word and deed to the power of Jesus's death and resurrection requires that we take Jesus's yoke upon ourselves. Belief without transformation—sadly, the experience of many people who would identify themselves as Christians—betrays a common misunderstanding among many evangelicals, namely, that it is possible to be a Christian without resembling Christ, without hating what he hates and loving what he loves, without following the Lamb "wherever he goes" (Rev 14:4). In this chapter, we look at the important theme of the yoke of Christ—that is, what it looks like to live under his rule, empowered by his Spirit.

An Easy Yoke—A Light Burden

A yoke is a frame to tie two animals together as they work a field. When used by a person, the yoke helps distribute weight evenly across the shoulders and facilitate transport. In the Old Testament, the metaphor of a yoke mainly denotes social or political oppression. It is an "unwelcome restriction."[3] So when Jesus invites us to take his yoke upon us, he's inviting us to a type of restriction. "Come to me, all of you who are weary and burdened, and I will give you rest. Take up my yoke and learn from me, because I am lowly and humble in heart, and you will find rest for your souls. For my yoke is easy and my burden is light" (Matt 11:28–30).

Jesus invites everyone to come to him, although there is a prerequisite. They must know they are weary and burdened. His point is not that some people are weary while others aren't, any more than he thinks some people need much forgiveness while others need little (Luke 7:47), or that some people are sick while others are healthy (Luke 5:31–32). His point is rather that a person will come to Jesus

---

[3] France, *Matthew*, 449 (see chap. 3, n. 4). The Mishnah speaks of the yoke of Torah (m. 'Abot 3:5).

only insofar as he or she realizes that life is wearisome and burdensome and that they need much forgiveness and healing because they are very sick.

So to people who feel burdened, Jesus offers not to take away their yoke altogether but to give them a new one. And the effect of his yoke is not a greater burden but rest—rest for their souls. His yoke is easy and his burden is light.[4] Again, his assumption is that humans always have a yoke and a burden. This assumption cuts against much modern thinking in which we are taught to believe that happiness and self-actualization happen when we are free—free from any external boundaries and ideas imposed upon us, and free to act according to our desires without censure or judgment. I am free if I can be myself. Autonomous.

But Jesus always comes with a yoke. He wants to help us see that there are no yoke-free people. The autonomous self is an illusion. The attempt to build our self from the ground up, guided by our intuitions and original thoughts, is itself a yoke and burden. It is crushing in scope, bankrupt from the start, and untethered to reality. Where do those intuitions and "original" thoughts come from, after all? Why are they so different if the person grew up in the mountain ranges of Thailand as opposed to the Upper West Side of Manhattan? Why do people of a particular place *share* a particular culture, an affinity for the same food, music, fashion, language, and ideas? We can't escape many of the traits and ways of thinking of the people around us. To be human is to be a cultural being, and our culture is itself a yoke with many positives and negatives.

Jesus offers a new yoke. "Take up my yoke and learn from me." The metaphor is *yoke*; the reality is "learn from me." Jesus in the Gospel of Matthew is presented to us as the teacher *par excellence*

---

[4] For an extended reflection on Jesus's yoke as rest, see John Mark Comer, *The Ruthless Elimination of Hurry* (Colorado Springs: WaterBrook, 2020).

whose words carry the authority and wisdom of God. His word stills storms, heals disease, exorcises evil spirits, forgives sin, and shapes the human soul. Learning is what a disciple does, which is why Jesus calls people to follow him. When we follow him, we learn to love what he loves and hate what he hates, but more importantly, we learn to love *him*. And love him, we must, for we become like the object of our love. His yoke and burden do not crush us because he is lowly and humble in heart. Think about how rare and refreshing is the posture of his heart. He has all authority in heaven and on earth, but he is lowly and humble in heart. And his teaching, his word, comes to us, not only externally in the Scriptures, but also internally by his Spirit. Remember: between his first and second coming, Jesus has sent us the Spirit of God, who is God within us.

A Revolutionary Concept and Reality

The mood and setting in the second half of John's Gospel changes significantly from the first. Starting in John 13, Jesus is no longer in the public eye doing mighty works and moving from town to town in the midst of clamoring crowds. He is in a private room preparing his twelve disciples for his departure. It is the week of his death.

Having spent a few years with them closely at his side, it was important to Jesus that his disciples understand that he would not leave them as orphans.

> If you love me, you will keep my commands. And I will ask the Father, and he will give you another Counselor to be with you forever. He is the Spirit of truth. The world is unable to receive him because it doesn't see him or know him. But you do know him, because he remains with you and will be in you.

I will not leave you as orphans; I am coming to you. (John
14:15–18)

The twelve disciples, with the exception of Judas the Betrayer,
had taken up Jesus's yoke. They had left everything to follow him.
They had come to know him better than anyone else. They had sat
under his teaching but also taken up his ministry as he sent them
out to preach and heal. And in the process of following him, they
had come to love him. Their love would be expressed through obedience. "If you love me, you will keep my commands." Just as his
presence had made it much easier for them to obey him, he lets them
know that after his departure he will send them "another Counselor,"
"the Spirit of truth," the Spirit who will remain with them and be *in*
them.[5]

This concept is revolutionary. Yet, more than a concept, it is a
reality. You will recall from the previous chapter that Moses asked
God to go with Israel on its journey, that apart from his presence
nothing distinguished Israel among the nations of the world. You
will recall that key events in Israel's history were the moments when
the glory of God filled the tabernacle and the temple. You will also
recall that Ezekiel had a vision of God's glory departing from the
temple. The temple was the place where God's presence dwelt. But
now Jesus was telling his distraught disciples that the Spirit of God
would remain with them and be in them. If Jesus is God with us, the
Spirit is God within us.

But Jesus also told his disciples that he had to first return to the
Father before he would send the Spirit. "It is for your benefit that I

---

[5]   Mark W. G. Stibbe, *John* (Sheffield, UK: Sheffield Academic, 1993), 154, says
of John 14:16, "His promise of 'another Counsellor' is really the promise of 'another
Jesus.'"

go away, because if I don't go away the Counselor will not come to you. If I go, I will send him to you" (John 16:7). Later, in Acts, when the Spirit came, the burden of Peter's sermon in Acts 2 was to prove to the people of Jerusalem—the ones who had witnessed and approved of Jesus's execution just seven weeks before—that Jesus, whom they had killed, was the one with authority from God to send the Spirit into the world. Peter told them that *in life* God had attested to Jesus's glory by the powerful works he had done; *in death* God loosed the pangs of death because it was impossible for death to keep a hold on Jesus; and *in resurrection* God enthroned Jesus to the highest place and gave him the promised Holy Spirit to send into the world (Acts 2:22–36).[6]

The coming of Jesus secured both the forgiveness of sins by his death and the sending of the Spirit by his resurrection and enthronement. No cross, no Spirit. No Spirit, no new life. Jesus's yoke is easy and his burden is light because he sends his own Spirit to dwell within us, and by his presence he transforms our lives and empowers our witness.

Presence and Power

The apostle Paul, perhaps more than any other New Testament writer, reflected on and penned down for us the inner workings of God's Spirit in the life of the believer. Paul found an antithesis at work in the world: the person of the flesh and the person of the Spirit.[7] The person of the flesh is hostile to God and does not submit

---

[6]   On the resurrection of Jesus Christ, see Gary R. Habermas and Michael R. Licona, *The Case for the Resurrection of Jesus Christ* (Grand Rapids: Kregel, 2004); N.T. Wright, *The Resurrection of the Son of God* (Minneapolis: Fortress, 2003).

[7]   Flesh here refers to a person who does not know God through Jesus Christ and is therefore dominated by sin.

to God's law; in fact, this person is unable to do so. But people of the Spirit walk according to the Spirit, have a mindset of life and peace, belong to Christ, and will have their mortal bodies raised to life (Rom 8:5–11).

Paul goes on to say, "If you live according to the flesh, you are going to die. But if by the Spirit you put to death the deeds of the body, you will live. For all those led by God's Spirit are God's sons" (vv. 13–14). I find Paul's explanation very helpful. There are "deeds of the body" that I must put to death. These are things that are contrary to the will of God. The Sermon on the Mount, in Matthew 5–7, gives a good sampling of such things. Likewise, Paul names many such activities, including sexual immorality, moral impurity, promiscuity, hatreds, strife, jealousy, outbursts of anger, selfish ambitions, factions, envy, drunkenness, and anything similar (see Gal 5:19–21). Behind every evil action that plagues our social, economic, and political structures, there is operative one or many of these practices.

Paul says I must put these things to death, but I do it by the Spirit's power. There is a volitional agency at work (I must do it) and a spiritual agency (the Spirit's presence and power within me enables me to do it). *If by the Spirit you put to death the deeds of the body, you will live.* In contrast, people without the Spirit of God have a double problem. They are hostile to God and unable to submit to him. But once they come to Jesus and take up his yoke—learn from him—they receive his forgiveness and his Spirit. His yoke is easy because his Spirit is truth and power, truth to unmask the deception of the deeds of the body and power to turn from them.

Many Christians feel utterly powerless to overcome sin. Addictions, of whatever type, feel like unbreakable chains.[8] Old patterns

---

[8]   A helpful book in understanding and overcoming addictions is Edward T. Welch, *Addictions: A Banquet in the Grave* (Phillipsburg, NJ: P&R, 2001).

in relationships lead to constant conflict. The victory of the cross seems to skip over life on the ground. But I want you to hear Paul's instruction again: "And if the Spirit of him who raised Jesus from the dead lives in you, then he who raised Christ from the dead will also bring your mortal bodies to life through his Spirit who lives in you" (Rom 8:11). We can't read over that statement too quickly. The same Spirit who raised Jesus from the dead lives in us and will give life to our mortal bodies. What the Spirit did for Jesus in death he will do for everyone who belongs to Jesus. And today, the Spirit is the presence and power of God in us, so that we may experience God's great love for us, a love that alone can transform us. "God's love has been poured out in our hearts through the Holy Spirit who was given to us" (Rom 5:5).

I encourage you. *Live by the power of the Spirit.* Imagine if John the Baptist had lied and one greater than John had never come, one who baptizes not with water but with the Holy Spirit and fire. We would have no power to change. We would lack the courage to speak up, the grace to show mercy, and the restraint to control our appetites. We would love ourselves and our kin but lack the inner motivation to love the stranger. But Jesus did come and the Spirit has been sent. And if his Spirit dwells in you, you have power. You will conquer. Your life will show it. Your love for God and people will grow. It's the miracle of the Christian faith.[9]

Humanity's Heavy Yoke

It would be helpful at this point to understand that our struggle to overcome sin is part of a larger, cosmic struggle that finds resolution

---

[9] For a greater understanding of the role of the Holy Spirit in the life of the believer, see Gordon D. Fee, *God's Empowering Presence: The Holy Spirit in the Letters of Paul* (Grand Rapids: Baker Academic, 1994). To take a deeper dive into the

and hope for the nations with the coming of Jesus. Psalm 2 begins with a question. "Why do the nations rage and the peoples plot in vain?" (v. 1). In the more than 2,500 intervening years since the writing of this psalm, not much has changed for the nations. They continue to rage. In the psalm, the nations rage against God and his anointed. "The kings of the earth take their stand, and the rulers conspire together against the LORD and his Anointed One: 'Let's tear off their chains and throw their ropes off of us'" (vv. 2–3). The authority of God and his chosen king in Jerusalem is perceived by the nations as chains and ropes, an unwelcome restriction that the peoples and their kings prefer to tear off. They want to emancipate themselves from God. What's so interesting for our purposes is that the word translated as "ropes" in the Greek text of Psalm 2:3 is the same Greek word translated as "yoke" in Matthew 11:29. The nations do not want the yoke of God, yet Jesus, the anointed son of God, says to everyone, "Take up my yoke and learn from me."

In Psalm 2, God responds to the nations' rage by asserting the following, "I have installed my king on Zion, my holy mountain" (v. 6). He then tells the people that his king will possess all the nations and that they should take warning and submit to him because "all who take refuge in him are happy" (v. 12). One scholar points out that nothing of the values of the king or of his kingship receives attention but only the king's threatening authority.[10] The nations despise the yoke of God, and God in return simply asserts his raw authority.

In the book of Revelation, a book that has many structural, thematic, and allusive similarities to Psalm 2,[11] there are two significant

theology of Paul, see Michael J. Gorman, *Apostle of the Crucified Lord: A Theological Introduction to Paul and His Letters*, 2nd ed. (Grand Rapids: Eerdmans, 2017).

[10] Luis A. Schökel and Cecilia Carniti, *Salmos I: Traducción, Introducciones y Comentario*, 3rd ed. (Estella, Navarra, Spain: Editorial Verbo Divino, 2002), 160.

[11] See Steve Moyise, "The Psalms in the Book of Revelation," in *The Psalms in the New Testament*, ed. Steve Moyise and M. J. J. Menken (London: T&T Clark,

developments that do speak to the king's values and the nature of his kingdom. The first is the king's love and death for his people. John writes, "To him who loves us and has set us free from our sins by his blood" (Rev 1:5b). This description comes right after John has introduced Jesus as "the ruler of the kings of the earth" (v. 5a). Jesus's universal authority over all nations and creatures, in heaven and on earth, permeates the Apocalypse, but right at the beginning John emphasizes Jesus's love for us, supremely demonstrated in his death to free us from our sins. In fact, the dominant image of Jesus in the Apocalypse is the Lamb—the Lamb who was slain. The crown on God's king is made of thorns.

The second development over the plotline of Psalm 2 comes in John's unveiling of the true source of the nations' chains and ropes. Similar to the way Psalm 2 begins, in Revelation 11 the nations rage in response to the announcement that the "kingdom of the world has become the kingdom of our Lord and of his Christ," his anointed (Rev 11:15, see v. 18). Once again, the nations are hostile to God. But then immediately after, in the second half of the book (Revelation 12–20), John offers a sustained depiction of the cosmic war in heaven and on earth, instigated by the Devil and his agents of evil. The intent of these forces of evil is to control and deceive the nations.[12]

On the one hand, John makes clear to the nations, the readers of the Apocalypse, that their chains and ropes—the yoke they want to throw off of themselves—come not from God but from their enemy, the Devil. On the other hand, he underscores that Jesus by his blood

---

2004), 231–6; Sam Janse, *"You Are My Son": The Reception History of Psalm 2 in Early Judaism and the Early Church* (Walpole, MA: Peeters, 2009), 131–4.

[12]   See Rev 13:7; 14:8; 17:15; 18:23; 20:3, 8, 10. For an in-depth development of John's story of the nations in Revelation, see Jon Morales, *Christ, Shepherd of the Nations: The Nations as Narrative Character and Audience in John's Apocalypse*, LNTS 577 (London: Bloomsbury T&T Clark, 2018).

has freed us from our sins. He came to die and thus wrest control away from the Devil, so that people everywhere might come under the light yoke of Jesus and find life.

> Then I heard a loud voice in heaven say,
> The salvation and the power
> and the kingdom of our God
> and the authority of his Christ
> have now come,
> because the accuser of our brothers and sisters,
> who accuses them
> before our God day and night,
> has been thrown down.
> They conquered him
> by the blood of the Lamb
> and by the word of their testimony;
> for they did not love their lives
> to the point of death. (Rev 12:10–11)

Like the rest of the New Testament, Revelation offers two alternatives: be under the oppressive yoke of the Devil or the light yoke of Jesus. Only one leads to true freedom. There is no third option. "If the Son sets you free, you really will be free" (John 8:36).

Listen to Him!

The yoke of Christ is none other than discipleship—learning from Jesus, following the Lamb wherever he goes, listening to his voice. Listening. The most basic obligation of the people of God is *listening*. "Listen, Israel: The LORD our God, the LORD is one" (Deut 6:4). "This is my beloved Son, with whom I am well-pleased.

Listen to him!" (Matt 17:5). From the inception of the church, the people of God have gathered together to receive the gospel in song, in preaching, in prayer, in the Lord's Supper, and in baptism. We hear God's Word with faith, and the Spirit of God transforms us into the likeness of God's Son.

Our fear must become love, which must become witness. As we learned at the beginning of this chapter, it is possible to be in the presence of greatness and be blind to it. This book has been an exercise in seeing because only when we experience the grandeur of God in Jesus are we able to love God by embracing his yoke and bear witness to his love to the ends of the earth. "They conquered him by the blood of the Lamb and the word of their testimony" (Rev 12:11).

In the final chapter we will explore the heart's greatest longing and Scripture's final vision—healing.

CHAPTER 6

Healing

A s I write this, my mother, only seventy-two years old, is dying. She has a rare degenerative disease called PSP (progressive supranuclear palsy). The illness has no known cause or cure. It affects brain function, so that the body slowly shuts down. First she began to lose her balance and fall. Then her eyesight grew dim. Then her speech slurred. Now she's having problems swallowing. She still sleeps well and really enjoys food—her last daily pleasure—but she also knows the day is coming when she won't be able to swallow.

My mother is a tenacious woman. Divorced, she raised six of us by herself in Colombia at the height of Pablo Escobar's drug cartel. My youngest brother was adopted when I was thirteen years old because he was in need and Mom has a big heart. She has always believed that where five can eat, so can six. Watching this force of nature reduced to a chair, in a room, unable to talk, saddens me and sobers me. Every human body is in a slow process of decay.

For the past two years, my sister's family and my family have taken turns, six months at a time, caring for Mom. During the most recent six-month season that Mom stayed at our home, we enjoyed the privilege of both hard and sweet moments. Her daily routine was generally the same. In the evenings, she would eat, brush her teeth, use the bathroom, and get in bed. This ritual could take two to three hours. When she finally lay down, most nights we would pray. I knew the whole time that our care was preparing her for life after death. On one particular night, I gave her a Bible verse that she latched on to the way a small child holds her blankie in the night. From that point forward, she would search for it, unable to remember it, completing it after I gave her the initial prompt. The verse was Philippians 1:21: "For me, to live is Christ and to die is gain." *Vivir es Cristo y morir es ganancia.* She felt ready, ready to wake up on the other side of life on earth. As her life ebbs away, she never complains but firmly believes that her body and soul will be made new at the resurrection of the righteous. She knows complete healing is on the way.

I Will Come and Heal Him

Healing is the deepest human need. The entire race, regardless of individual achievement, bows before the fury of disease and death. For this reason, when Jesus walked on earth, the bulk of his ministry was taken up by teaching and healing. Both his power and willingness to heal were evident.

In the episode with the Roman centurion, one of the few narrated interactions between Jesus and a Gentile (a non-Jewish person), I'm struck by Jesus's readiness to help him. The centurion said, "Lord, my servant is lying at home paralyzed, in terrible agony," and Jesus replies, "I will come and heal him" (Matt 8:6–7 CSB note). That's it. No preamble. No triage. No questions asked. *I will come and heal him.* Interestingly, in Luke's version of the episode, the centurion sent elders of the Jews to make the request on his behalf, and they tried to persuade Jesus to come by saying, "He is worthy for you to grant this, because he loves our nation and has built us a synagogue" (Luke 7:4–5). But when Jesus was on the way, the centurion reversed the statement of the elders by sending friends who said on his behalf, "Lord, don't trouble yourself, since I am not worthy to have you come under my roof" (Luke 7:6). Worthiness, or lack thereof, did not matter. What mattered was that a friend was sick, and the centurion believed Jesus could heal him. That, in fact, is the deeper point of the episode—the trust of the centurion in Jesus's authority to heal.

It would take many pages to detail all the accounts in the Gospels of Jesus's healings. The evangelists themselves did not have the pages needed to record every instance Jesus healed. They availed themselves of summary statements such as this one: "Jesus continued going around to all the towns and villages, teaching in their synagogues, preaching the good news of the kingdom, and healing every disease and every sickness" (Matt 9:35). Or: "And there are also many other things that Jesus did, which, if every one of them were written down, I suppose not even the world itself could contain the books that would be written" (John 21:25). The power and willingness of Jesus to heal brought relief to countless faces, amazed the crowds, enraged his opponents, and convinced his followers that he was the deliverer sent from God.

Try Harder? Be Smarter?

There is a conundrum found in Scripture as in life. How can I become good when I'm not good? How can I become loving toward someone I hate? How can an addict turn from addiction? We've all heard the simplistic answer: *Try harder. Be smarter.* Judging by the chaos and brokenness around us, we all must be incorrigible weaklings and very slow.

In Scripture, the conundrum is stated this way: "Blessed are the pure in heart, for they will see God" (Matt 5:8). To see God, my heart must be pure. But, according to Jesus, the things that defile a person come from the heart: "But what comes out of the mouth comes from the heart, and this defiles a person. For from the heart come evil thoughts, murders, adulteries, sexual immoralities, thefts, false testimonies, slander" (Matt 15:18–19). Elsewhere he says that we humans are evil (Matt 7:11). So the conundrum is that in order to see God I need a pure heart, but what I have instead is a defiled and defiling heart. How do I find a way out? Try harder? Be smarter?

There is another passage in Matthew that solves the mystery.

> Isaiah's prophecy is fulfilled in them, which says:
> You will listen and listen,
> but never understand;
> you will look and look,
> but never perceive.
> For this people's heart
> has grown callous;
> their ears are hard of hearing,
> and they have shut their eyes;
> otherwise they might see
> with their eyes,
> and hear with their ears, and
> understand with their hearts,
> and turn back—and I would heal them. (Matt 13:14–15)

There is gold here! Matthew, quoting Isaiah, is saying that we're so sick, so blind to the things of God, so deaf that we barely hear them. But Matthew also casts his Gospel, from the very beginning and as it unfolds, as a story of fulfillment. The Son of God, the Messiah, has been sent to us and he has done what has never been done before, taught with authority never heard before, and died with a love never seen before. He's a divine magnet, in human form—so powerful, true, and beautiful, that when we see him (blind as we are), hear him (deaf as we are), and understand him with our hearts (callous as we are), we turn back. All we have to do in the presence of the divine magnet that is Jesus is turn to him. *He does the healing*. The Son of God has come and loved us in his life, death, and resurrection, and the magnet of that love pulls us toward him that he might heal us. "By his wounds you have been healed" (1 Pet 2:24). Jesus not only heals our illnesses, but also our hearts. This is the wonder of the Christian faith found in no other religion or philosophical system. God justifies the wicked. Jesus heals the sick heart.

Healing the Nations

The last word on the nations in the entire Bible is a word of hope. "The tree of life was on each side of the river, bearing twelve kinds of fruit, producing its fruit every month. The leaves of the tree are for healing the nations" (Rev 22:2). John's knowledge of Scripture was encyclopedic, and he made ample use of it as he penned down the vision Jesus gave him through the angel. The Scriptures, particularly the Hebrew Bible, formed his vocabulary, but the ideas he put in writing always served the universal scope of Jesus's mission.

Many centuries before Jesus, the prophet Ezekiel had seen a vision of a river with many fruit trees growing on each side. "Their fruit will serve for food and their leaves for medicine" (Ezek 47:12). Similarly, in the new creation, John saw a river flowing from the throne of God and of the Lamb, and on either side of the river there was a tree, the tree of life. Unlike Ezekiel, John did not simply say that the tree's leaves are for healing. John saw that the leaves of the tree are "for healing the nations."

Ponder this with me. John in Revelation endeavors to show how the nations of the world are under the tyranny and dominion of

Babylon, a metaphor that describes Rome's political, economic, and religious oppression of the nations and peoples in the Empire. Moreover, John also unveils how Babylon itself is under the dominion of the Devil and his agents.[1] So the chain of oppression runs like this: the Devil and his agents over Babylon; Babylon over the nations. But even more important than this reign of terror is John's narration of the role God, Jesus, and the church play in the nations' liberation. John sees the dazzling throne of God, who is king of the nations, whose throne is greater than Satan's throne, and whose ways are just and true. He sees Jesus, the Son of God who loves us and purchased by his blood people for God from every nation. And he also sees the church, who by her purity and witness shepherds the nations under delegated authority from Christ.[2] In this way, Revelation unveils not only the deceptive yoke of the Devil but also the redemptive presence of God. When the nations see what John has seen—the Lamb who was slain to achieve the nations' freedom ("To him who loves us and has set us free from our sins by his blood," Rev 1:5)—they will turn to God in worship.

Such was the prophet's hope for the nations. To be able to turn and be healed, they needed to see the true nature of reality. The leaves of the tree of life are "for healing the nations." Not death and judgment but healing and life bring the biblical canon to a close. God declares, "Look, I am making everything new" (Rev 21:5). The question for all individuals from the nations is whether they, like John, will see their dilemma in the grip of evil supernatural powers

---

[1]   Revelation 17:15–16 says, "The waters you saw, where the prostitute was seated, are peoples, multitudes, nations, and languages. The ten horns you saw, and the beast, will hate the prostitute." The prostitute is Babylon and the image of "sitting" (over nations) is an image of domination. Further, Babylon says, "I sit as queen" (Rev 18:7), a statement that rivals God, who sits on the throne (see Rev 4:2–3, 9–10; 5:1, 7, 13; 6:16; 7:10, 15; 19:4; 20:11; 21:5). See Morales, *Christ, Shepherd*, 109–23.

[2]   See Morales, *Christ, Shepherd*, 137–46.

but also with the Creator God, Jesus the Lamb who was slain, and the witnessing church on their side. Will they wash their robes and make them white in the blood of the Lamb (Rev 7:14)?

The Good Virus

The church is the instrument by which the healing of the slaughtered Lamb spreads throughout the earth. For this reason, the church must preserve her distinct witness in word and deed to the restorative power of God, rather than lose it by assimilation. Assimilation—adopting the values, beliefs, and behaviors of the culture around us—has always been a challenge for the church because human beings have a strong need to belong. We imitate how people around us dress, talk, and behave.

I remember when I attended New York University. I would pass by the Stern School of Business and notice that all the students would be dressed in suits. It was the strangest thing. Everybody, twenty-year-olds like myself, would be standing outside smoking and hanging out, wearing expensive business suits. The reason was that these students aspired to work on Wall Street, and that's how people in those sectors dressed. So the school wanted the students to assimilate to the industry standards right from the beginning. As for me and my classmates at Tisch School of the Arts, we wore ripped jeans and T-shirts. Why? Because most aspiring actors end up working in restaurants anyway. We fit right in.

Some cultural practices do not clash with the witness of the church. Others do, and it is in those instances that our allegiance to Jesus is tested. Take food sacrificed to idols, an issue that comes up in Corinthians, Acts, and Revelation. Gentile Christians in the Roman Empire grew up and lived in a context where worship of the gods and worship of the emperor were woven into the fabric of civic life. It was standard practice for a Roman citizen or resident to write vows on a tablet, take it to the pagan temple, set it on the statue of the god, and have the priests there kill an animal as a sacrificial offering. The organs and entrails were burnt as an offering to the god, and the meat was shared with family and friends, right there in the temple. Meat, however, was rare. Only the wealthy ate it with any regularity. So a person who received an invitation to a sacrifice ritual would want to go just for the meat! But the whole affair was religious in nature. There's even evidence of the statue of a god being brought into the dining hall, symbolizing the presence of the god. In addition to sacrificial offerings, there were also many festivals to the gods, which went on for days and included sexual relations.[3]

Imagine the pressure on the Christians to assimilate to these practices. Imagine that the people at your job were going for food and drinks after work to wrap up a business deal, and you knew that at the restaurant everyone would raise a glass to Artemis or Serapis or some other god. What would you do if you were a Christian? Would you say to yourself, "I don't really believe these are gods anyway, so it doesn't matter. I'll just pay lip service"? This kind of approach is the very thing that false teachers advocated and Jesus opposes, for example, in Revelation 2:12–17. Or maybe you would decline every time because you knew you could not engage in such practices with a clear conscience. But now you become a target, the questions start coming, and you start losing business opportunities.

This failure to participate in civic life is one of the reasons Christians in the early centuries of the faith were accused of being haters of the human race. They refused to show political loyalty to the Roman emperor and the gods—the ones who were thought to

---

[3] For more information on Roman pagan sacrifices and their impact on the early Christian communities, see Ben Witherington III, "Not So Idle Thoughts about *Eidolothuton*," *Tyndale Bulletin* 44, no. 2 (1993): 237–54.

preserve order, peace, and prosperity—and, thus, to the Roman people. Christians were seen as a danger to the social order, treasonous indeed, and many chose the path of assimilation. Avoid trouble. Blend in.

The challenge for the church today (as it was for the early Gentile Christians) is that we belong to our culture. We wear skinny jeans and drink ventis and post pictures of ourselves doing the silliest things because that's what our culture does. We've imbibed our culture, which really does have many wonderful things—from art to food to technology that eases and even saves human life. The companies and institutions you work for probably have some great mission statements and values. We have used our minds and passions to increase justice and peace on the earth. But there are also deadly things about our culture. There are values, beliefs, and behaviors that are set against God and permeate all institutions, companies, and households. No institution and no person is all bad or all good. We all still bear the image of God, but we all bear that image marred, stained, and disfigured by sin.

The beauty and power of the gospel is that Jesus Christ is, as C. S. Lewis put it, the good virus. As people receive him by faith, he begins to remake us. He forgives us and begins to heal us from the effects of sin. We are able to move into the world bearing his love and sharing his name, so that his good contagion covers the earth, all the while knowing that neither we nor the world will be fully healed or remade until his return.

This is why, if we're going to make an eternal difference on earth, we must fully identify with Jesus and his people.[4] We must be trained by his word in the community of believers, so that we have

---

[4] For a thoughtful reflection on the hospitality that Christians as a community of Christ followers should offer, see Rosaria Butterfield, *The Gospel Comes with a House Key* (Wheaton: Crossway, 2018).

the discernment to know the things in our culture that we must say no to and the ones we can affirm. Otherwise, if by our lifestyle and teaching we resemble the world more than the Christ, we lose our witness and Jesus himself will come and make war against us by the sword of his mouth (Rev 2:16). But if we receive his forgiveness, belong to his people, live empowered by his presence, and take up his yoke—the themes highlighted in this book—we experience the healing of the age to come and become agents of healing in a world that is desperately sick yet unable to name the malaise.

When God Makes All Things New

When I was growing up, no one in my family was a Christian. I moved to New York City at the age of eighteen and became a Christian two months later. The kindness of God—I was totally lost in a small city of Colombia and wonderfully saved (and safe) in the Big Apple. After many years, some family members came to Christ. One of them was Mom. She spent most of her life under the heavy yoke of sin and of social forces that erode our humanity and steal our dignity. But the great thing about Jesus is that the new life he gives is as true for latecomers as for everyone else because it's not based on our track record. Our good deeds can't get us in, nor can our bad deeds keep us out. What matters is that we trust the death of Jesus for the forgiveness of our sins and trust his resurrection as the firstfruits of our own resurrection when God makes all things new.

Mom says, "The Lord has taught me a lot through this illness. I thank him for it." The highest lessons often come when the soul is brought low. Mom's illness has no cure—until she takes her last breath. I tell her, as she sits in her wheelchair, "One day you're going to be running!" She knows. Complete healing, of body and soul, is on the way.[5]

---

[5]   Mom went home to glory on July 9, 2020.

Epilogue: People as Trees

We began with the story of six blind men. We ended with six big themes of the Bible.[1] We also looked at the blind man in the Gospel of Mark who, upon the first touch of Jesus to his eyes, saw people but they looked like trees. The man becomes a parable of our impaired eyesight. Adam and Eve took and ate of the tree God had forbidden, and they lost their spiritual sight. Only the coming of Jesus with his offer to take and eat of his body on the tree, the cross, gives us life and restores our sight. His offer extends to all the nations. "The leaves of the tree are for healing the nations" (Rev 22:2).

The most prevalent yet most toxic form of religion and philosophy in the world is the one that says, *Do this and you will live.* Twelve, ten, seven rules for life. The yoke is heavy, and we always fail. Unfortunately, much of the Christian church has done no better. After all, God did give us ten commandments, and Jesus did not relax them.

So let's rehearse this one more time. Jesus said, "In the same way, every good tree produces good fruit, but a bad tree produces bad fruit. A good tree can't produce bad fruit; neither can a bad tree produce good fruit. Every tree that doesn't produce good fruit is cut

---

[1] My thanks to Cor Bennema, who noticed the parallel of six blind men and six big themes. Though seeing, I do not see!

down and thrown into the fire. So you'll recognize them by their fruit" (Matt 7:17–20). In the metaphor, people are trees, good or bad, and they produce good or bad fruit. And what Jesus is looking for—let's not be confused—is good fruit. *But the fruit comes second.* First comes the tree. And how does the tree become good and healthy? We saw it in the last chapter. We turn to Jesus, and he does the healing.

Each of the big themes in this book—creation, forgiveness, people, presence, yoke, and healing—captures important aspects of the story of God and his good purposes for creation. Other themes could have been chosen. My goal in this short book was to help you see more of Jesus Christ as he's revealed to us in some of the big themes of the Bible. Upon seeing him, I pray that you find yourself happily as one whose robes have been washed and made white in the blood of the Lamb.

Name and Subject Index

A

abortion   *50*

Abraham   *40–42*

aseity   *12*

assimilation   *95–98*

B

baptism   *55, 67, 88*

Bauckham, Richard   *19, 71*

Bird, Michael F.   *13*

blindness

  spiritual   *3–6*

Bonhoeffer, Dietrich   *55*

Bridges, Jerry   *16*

C

Carniti, Cecilia   *85*

church   *17–18, 39, 42, 55, 57, 59,*
    77, 88, 94–95, 97, 99

circumcision   *45*

covenant

  new   *55–57*

  rescinded   *47*

  with Abraham   *44–45*

  with David   *46–47*

  with Israel   *45–46*

creation   *9–22*

  Father, Son, Spirit in   *12–13*

  new   *16–19*

Creator-creature distinction   *13,*
    20–21

D

debt   *36–37*

deception   *25–29, 83, 86*

Devil   *25–29, 34, 86–87, 94*

E

eating   *26–27, 31–33, 56*

Enns, Peter   *62*

Epcot   *48*

Epstein, Greg M.   *35*

F

faith   *60*

fall of humankind   *25–31*

family

  of God   *52–55*

  of origin   *53*

Fee, Gordon D.   *84*

Ferry, Luc   *25*

forgiveness   *23–37*

  accomplishing   *36*

  meaning of   *35*

  need of   *35*

Frame, John   *20, 34*

France, R. T.   *51, 78*

G

Gentry, Peter J.   *47*

God

as creator   *10–14*

as father   *49–52*

coming of   *69–71*

friendship of   *61–62*

glory of   *64–66, 82*

judgment of   *31–32, 35*

name of   *64–65*

presence of   *59–73*

worship of   *63*

good deeds

motivation for

Gorman, Michael J.   *19, 34, 85*

Grudem, Wayne   *25*

Guillen, Michael   *11*

H

Habermas, Gary R.   *82*

healing   *69–70, 89–98*

heart

spiritually sick   *91–93*

Hellerman, Joseph H.   *55*

Hurtado, Larry W.   *71*

I

idolatry   *61*

individualism   *39–40, 42–43, 53*

Israel

formation of   *40–47*

J

Janse, Sam   *86*

Jesus

agent in creation   *12–13*

and the storm   *59–60, 70–71*

as food   *33, 35–36*

as God with us   *67–73*

as good virus   *97*

as Immanuel   *67–68*

as narrator   *4, 7*

baptism of   *13*

blood of   *56, 86–87*

coming of   *21, 68–71, 82,
84–87, 99*

death of   *6, 13, 21, 33, 56, 72,
77–78, 80, 82, 84, 86, 93,
98*

encountering   *48*

family of   *52–55*

feet of   *23*

following   *54, 76–78, 80–81*

glory of   *75–77*

healings of   *4–5, 69–70, 90–91,
99*

identity of   *5–7 , 71*

in Revelation   *18–19, 72, 76–77,
85–87, 93–95*

kingship of   *84–87*

listening to   *53–55, 87–88*

ministry to women   *23–24*

mission of   *39, 55–57*

resurrection of   *13, 72, 78, 82, 93, 98*

revealing the Father   *49–52*

yoke of   *78–80*

K

Kupp, David D.   *68*

L

Lewis, C. S.   *50, 97*

Licona, Michael R.   *82*

Lord's Prayer   *39–40, 48–50*

Lord's Supper   *33, 36, 88*

love

in relation to forgiveness   *24–25, 36–37*

M

MacIntyre, Alasdair   *50*

Menken, M. J. J.   *85*

Moyise, Steve   *85*

N

nations   *15–17, 19–20, 67, 85–86, 93–95, 99*

Nicene Creed   *20*

O

obedience   *80–81*

P

Pennington, Jonathan T.   *52*

Piper, John   *34*

Plantinga, Alvin   *50*

providence   *14–16, 21*

R

rebellion   *28–29, 35, 47–48, 61, 63*

religion   *51*

rest   *79*

Revelation   *17–19, 48, 72, 78–79, 85–88, 93–96, 98–99*

Robertson, O. Palmer   *47*

Roberts, Vaughan   *41*

S

sacrifice

animal   *63*

Roman   *95–96*

Schökel, Luis A.   *85*

seed   *40*

seeing   *3–6, 24, 70, 88, 99–100*

Shema   *20*

sin   *35, 83*

Sire, James W.   *14*

Spirit, Holy   *80–84*

steady-state hypothesis   *11*

Stibbe, Mar W. G.   *81*

storm   *70–71*

as metaphor for trials   *59–60*

T

tabernacle   *63–64*

Taylor, Charles   *50*

temple   *64–66, 68*

transgression   *31–32*

Trinity   *12–14, 68*

trust   *90–91, 98*

U

unbelief   *18–19*

V

Van Til, Cornelius   *20*

W

Waltke, Bruce K.   *11*

Watson, Francis   *12*

Weingarten, Gene   *75*

Welch, Edward T.   *83*

Wellum, Stephen J.   *47*

world   *50*

worship   *11, 34, 39, 47, 61, 66, 72, 94–96*

Wright, Christopher J. H.   *72*

Wright, N. T.   *33, 72, 82*

Scripture Index

Genesis

1   *12, 14, 25*
1:1   *10*
1:2   *12*
1–3   *10*
1:3   *12*
1:27   *9*
2:16   *27*
2:16–17   *26*
2:17   *27*
2:24   *9*
2:25   *29*
3   *19, 25*
3:1–7   *26*
3:3   *27*
3:4   *28*
3:5   *28*
3:6   *28, 33*
3:8   *30–31*
3:9   *31*
3:9–19   *31*
3:15   *40*
3:17–18   *32*
4:25   *40*
11   *47*
12   *44*
12:1–3   *41*
15   *44*

15:18   *44*
17   *44*
17:1–8   *45*
17:10–11   *45*
17:17   *45*
22   *44*

Exodus

9:16   *42*
19:5–6   *45*
20:3   *54*
20:4–5   *61*
32   *47*
33   *62*
33:3   *61*
33:11   *62*
33:14   *61*
33:15   *61*
33:16   *62*
33:17–18   *61*
33:19   *62*
34:6–7   *14*
40:33–38   *63*

Numbers

13–14   *47*

Deuteronomy

6:4   *20, 87*
12:11   *64*

2 Samuel

7:11–16 *46*

1 Kings

8 *64*

8:10–11 *64*

8:27 *65*

8:29 *64*

8:33 *64*

8:35 *64*

8:41–42 *65*

8:44 *65*

9:6–7 *66*

Job

5:18 *48*

33:4 *12*

Psalms

2 *85–86*

2:1 *85*

2:2–3 *85*

2:6 *85*

2:12 *85*

33 *15*

33:5 *15*

33:10–22 *15–16*

104:30 *12*

107 *71*

107:23–30 *70–71*

Isaiah

1 *47*

35:3–6 *69*

40:3–5 *68*

40–55 *69*

53:4 *56*

53:5 *56*

60:1–3 *66*

Ezekiel

11:23 *66*

47:12 *93*

Hosea

1:9 *47*

2:23 *48*

Matthew

1:21 *33, 55*

1:23 *67*

3:3 *68*

4:2–3 *34*

4:4 *34*

4:10 *34*

5:3–10 *50*

5–7 *83*

5:8 *91*

5:16 *51*

5:21–48 *51*

5:44–45 *51*

5:45 *16*

6:4 *52*

6:6 *52*

6:9 *21*

6:9–13 *39, 49*

6:18 *52*

6:26 *16*

7:11 *92*

7:17–20 *99*

8:6–7 *90*

8:17 *56*

8:27 *60, 70*

9:1–8 *56*

9:35 *91*

11:28–30 *78*

13:14–15 *92*

15:18–19 *92*

15:29–31 *70*

17:5 *88*

18:19–20 *67*

19:4 *9*

19:5 *9*

26:26–28 *33, 56*

28:18–20 *67*

28:19 *20*

Mark

1:3 *68*

3:33–35 *53*

4:39 *59*

4:40 *60*

4:41 *60, 71*

8:14–18 *5*

8:23–25 *4*

8:29 *6*

9:7 *54*

10:19 *54*

10:21 *54*

Luke

3:4–6 *68*

5 *76*

5:5 *76*

5:8 *76*

5:10–11 *76*

5:31–32 *78*

7:4–5 *90*

7:6 *91*

7:37–38 *23*

7:41–42 *36*

7:41–43 *24*

7:44–48 *24*

7:47 *78*

8:25 *60*

John

1:1 *12*

1:3 *13*

1:23 *68–69*

4:31 *34*

4:32 *34*

4:34 *34*

6:51 *35–36*

8:36 *87*

14:15–18 *81*

14:16 *81*

16:7 *82*

21:25 *91*

Acts

2 *82*

2:22–36 *82*

Romans

5:5   *84*

8:5–11   *83*

8:11   *84*

8:13–14   *83*

Galatians

5:19–21   *83*

Ephesians

3:17–19   *55*

Philippians

1:21   *90*

Colossians

1:16   *13*

Hebrews

1:2   *13*

9:22   *46*

11   *43*

11:39–12:1   *43*

James

2:23   *41*

1 Peter

2:24   *33, 93*

3:18   *21*

2 Peter

2:4   *25*

Revelation

1:5   *86, 94*

1:5a   *86*

1:11   *77*

1:12–16   *77*

1:17–19   *77*

1:18   *18*

2:1   *18*

2–3   *18*

2:7   *19*

2:11   *19*

2:12–17   *96*

2:16   *98*

2:17   *19*

2:26–27   *19*

3:5   *19*

3:12   *19*

3:21   *19*

4:2–3   *94*

4:9–10   *94*

5:1   *94*

5:5   *18*

5:7   *94*

5:13   *94*

6:16   *94*

7:10   *94*

7:14   *95*

7:15   *94*

11   *86*

11:15   *86*

11:18   *86*

12:10–11   *87*

12–20   *86*

13:7   *86*

14:4   *78*

14:8   *86*

17:15   *86*

17:15–16   *94*

18:7   *94*

18:23   *86*

19:4   *94*

20   *19*

20:3   *86*

20:8   *86*

20:10   *86*

20:11   *94*

21:1   *19*

21:1–5   *17*

21:3   *19, 72*

21:5   *19, 94*

22:2   *93, 99*